The Lance Mackey Story

How My Obsession with Dog Mushing Saved My Life

By Lance Mackey

Foreword by Joe Runyan

Zorro Books
Fairbanks, Alaska

ISBN 978-0-615-35471-2

Library of Congress Control Number: 2001012345

FIRST PRINTING: February 2010
SECOND PRINTING: August 2010

CONTRIBUTING EDITOR: Joe Runyan
PROJECT EDITOR: Tricia Brown
ILLUSTRATOR: Jon Van Zyle
DESIGNER/MAPMAKER: Kitty Herrin, Arrow Graphics
EDITORIAL ASSISTANTS: Tonya Mackey, Theresa Daily

PRINTED BY: Friesens Inc., Altona, Manitoba, Canada

Zorro Books
An imprint of Zorro Books, LLC
Lance Mackey and Joe Runyan, owners
P.O. Box 10262
Fairbanks, Alaska 99710
(907) 688-3562
www.mackeyscomebackkennel.com / mackeykennel@gmail.com

Distributed by Zorro Books LLC

Front cover: *Lance Mackey and team, five miles from the finish line in the 2007 Iditarod Trail Sled Dog Race.* JEFF SCHULTZ / ALASKASTOCK. Inset photo: *Leaders Larry and Lippy shared the spotlight in the 2007 Iditarod win.* Map photo inset: *Under the Iditarod's Burled Arch with Maple and Larry, following a third straight victory in 2009.* THERESA DAILY PHOTO. Back cover: *Lance Mackey poses with an armful of Iditarod and Quest hopefuls.* THERESA DAILY PHOTO. Inset: *Mackey's famous leaders—Zorro, Larry, and Lippy—each have a following. A Mackey friend with a sense of humor, Sarida Steed-Bradley designed popular patches that honor these dogs.*

Iditarod® and Iditarod Trail Sled Dog Race® are registered trademarks of the Iditarod Trail Committee, Inc.

To Angel,
a very special Alaskan Husky,
who met me inside the walls of a hospital room,
then led me out to the wide, open trail.

ACKNOWLEDGMENTS

The list of my many friends and sponsors who have inspired and supported me is a book of its own. You all have a place in my heart.

The incredible journey of my life would not have been possible without the support and love of my family: my devoted wife, Tonya; my wonderful parents; my amazing children, Amanda, Brittney and Cain; and my hardworking handler, Braxton.

A special thanks to my collaborators and partners on this project: Joe Runyan, a fellow musher and friend who understands my life with sled dogs. Together, we organized hours of tapes, interviews, and old memories and condensed them into a book. Tricia Brown, editor, who molded the written and visual elements into a publishable work; Jon Van Zyle for enriching the text with his magical artwork; Kitty Herrin for designing such a beautiful book; the talented photographers who shared their wonderful photos; and Theresa Daily, our dear friend, who worked tirelessly to collect archival photos, audiotapes, and biographical material for the book.

Without all of these individuals, *The Lance Mackey Story* would have never found its way from my head to the written page.

I'm a lucky musher.

CONTENTS

	Alaska Race Circuit map	vi–vii
Foreword	THE INCREDIBLE LANCE MACKEY by Joe Runyan	ix
Chapter 1	A DREAM STATE	1
Chapter 2	BORN TO MUSH	7
Chapter 3	WILD CHILD	17
Chapter 4	THE COLDFOOT 'SOLUTION'	26
Chapter 5	FROM THE ARCTIC CIRCLE TO THE HIGH SEAS	32
Chapter 6	DANGEROUS LIVING ON THE BERING SEA	38
Chapter 7	THE TURNAROUND	46
Chapter 8	BUILDING A 'REAL' DOG TEAM	55
Chapter 9	AN EYE ON THE BIG LEAGUE	63
Chapter 10	MY ROOKIE RUN	69
Chapter 11	AFTERMATH	76
Chapter 12	YEAR TWO OF 'THE PLAN'	87
Chapter 13	COMEBACK KENNEL	99
Chapter 14	A FURIOUS CAMPAIGN OF RACING	107
Chapter 15	I KEEP A VOW	115
Chapter 16	DOG CARE, MY CARE	125
Chapter 17	'MY EXPECTATION IS TO WIN BOTH'	137
Chapter 18	AN IMPOSSIBLE TRIUMPH	150
Chapter 19	AND AGAIN IN 2008	166
Chapter 20	GOOD DOG	183
Chapter 21	CAN IT BE DONE AGAIN?	199
Chapter 22	2009 RACE MODE AND MY TEAM	210
Chapter 23	INTO THE STORM WITH LARRY	223
Chapter 24	VIEW FROM THE DOG YARD	245
	Race Record	259
	Special Awards	262

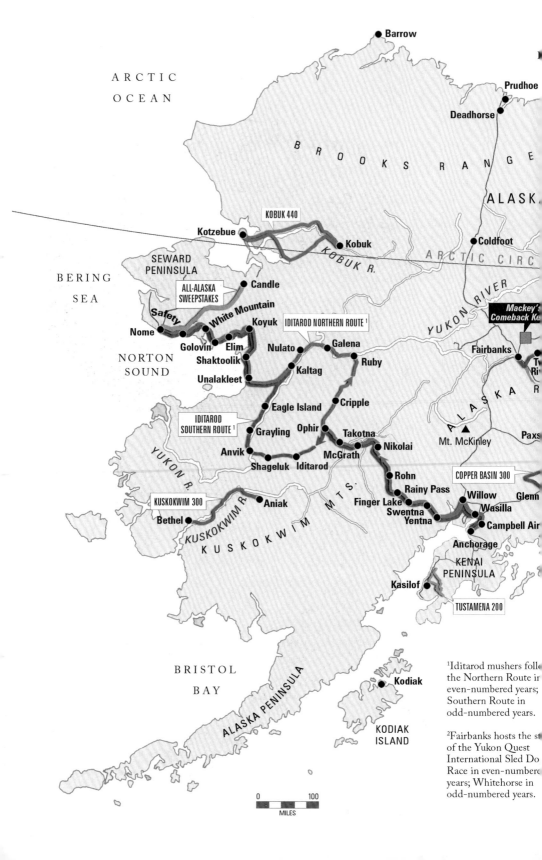

Barrow

Prudhoe

Deadhorse

ARCTIC
OCEAN

BROOKS RANGE

ALASKA

Coldfoot

KOBUK 440

Kotzebue

Kobuk

ARCTIC CIRCLE

KOBUK R.

YUKON RIVER

BERING
SEA

SEWARD
PENINSULA

Candle

Mackey's
Comeback Ke

ALL-ALASKA
SWEEPSTAKES

White Mountain

Safety

Koyuk

IDITAROD NORTHERN ROUTE [1]

Fairbanks

T
Ri

Nome

Golovin Elim

Nulato

Galena

NORTON
SOUND

Shaktoolik

Kaltag

Ruby

Unalakleet

Eagle Island

Cripple

A L A S K A R

IDITAROD
SOUTHERN ROUTE [1]

Grayling

Ophir

Takotna

Paxs

Anvik

McGrath

Nikolai

Mt. McKinley

Shageluk

Iditarod

KUSKOKWIM 300

Aniak

Bethel

KUSKOKWIM R.

Rohn

COPPER BASIN 300

Rainy Pass

Finger Lake

Willow

Glenn

Swentna

Wasilla

Yentna

Campbell Air

KUSKOKWIM MTS.

Anchorage

KENAI
PENINSULA

YUKON R.

Kasilof

TUSTAMENA 200

BRISTOL

Kodiak

BAY

KODIAK
ISLAND

ALASKA PENINSULA

[1]Iditarod mushers foll
the Northern Route in
even-numbered years;
Southern Route in
odd-numbered years.

[2]Fairbanks hosts the st
of the Yukon Quest
International Sled Do
Race in even-numbere
years; Whitehorse in
odd-numbered years.

0   100
MILES

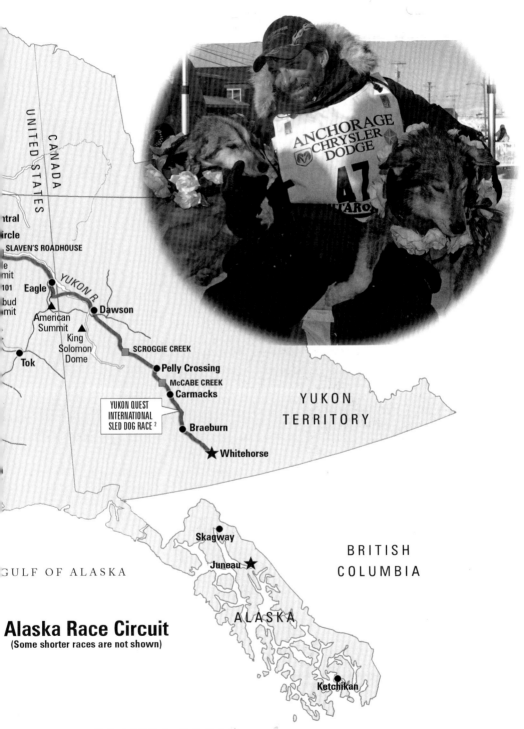

ORT   SEA

CANADA

UNITED STATES

ntral
ircle
SLAVEN'S ROADHOUSE
le
mit
101   Eagle
bud
mit
        American
        Summit
Tok   King
        Solomon
        Dome

YUKON R.

Dawson

SCROGGIE CREEK

Pelly Crossing

McCABE CREEK

Carmacks

YUKON QUEST
INTERNATIONAL
SLED DOG RACE ²

Braeburn

★ Whitehorse

YUKON

TERRITORY

Skagway

GULF OF ALASKA

Juneau ★

BRITISH

COLUMBIA

ALASKA

Alaska Race Circuit
(Some shorter races are not shown)

Ketchikan

PACIFIC OCEAN

The finish line of 2007 was sweet, both for winning the world's two biggest races back-to-back, but also wearing bib number 13—a lucky number for Alaska's first family of mushing. JEFF SCHULTZ / ALASKASTOCK

FOREWORD **THE INCREDIBLE LANCE MACKEY**

Lance Mackey first caught my attention while I was covering the 2001 Iditarod as a television commentator and trail reporter. He was a sound-bite machine, bright-eyed, quick-smiling, fast-moving, exuberant, lithe, lean, and athletic. He was also the son of the 1978 Iditarod champ Dick Mackey, and the younger brother of 1983 Iditarod and 1996 Yukon Quest champ Rick Mackey. Dick and Rick, the only father and son to win the Iditarod—at that time—were friends, fellow mushers, and neighbors of mine in Nenana, Alaska.

But who was Lance Mackey, the thirty-one-year-old rookie in his first Iditarod? And with the genetics of an Iditarod musher, why hadn't I seen him racing before? I got to know him a lot better over the next nine years.

Lance Mackey, I was to discover, is one of those rare, resolute humans who has been molded, hammered, pummeled, shaped, and unmercifully reduced by life and circumstance—only to emerge again as a bright star for all who surround him. You'll soon read the details of his remarkable personal story in this book—his battle with addictions, his knock-down, no-holds fights with cancer, and his comeback with a vengeance for life.

But I cannot resist the opportunity to state his accomplishments in the sled-dog world of long-distance mushing. Lance will fail to adequately blow his own horn.

Surprising for those who live in urban and temperate environments, mushing is widely practiced in Alaska and Canada, but also across the northern-tier states, Asia, South America, Russia, and Europe.

Norwegian musher Robert Sørlie, for example, won the Iditarod Trail Sled Dog Race in 2003 and 2005. Hundreds of thousands embrace the sport around the world.

Wilderness racing with sled dogs attracts ardent adventurers with a keen sense of competition. In the far-flung community of mushers is a certain recognition of the Iditarod Trail Sled Dog Race, the 1,100-mile race from Anchorage to Nome, as the pre-eminent long-distance race. The Yukon Quest International Sled Dog Race, between Whitehorse and Fairbanks, is highly regarded as the second most prestigious race at 1,000 miles. To win either is an accomplishment.

Several mushers have won both races, but in different years. I was the first to win both races, followed by Rick Mackey (Lance's brother), and Jeff King of Denali Park, Alaska. It's fair to say that Rick, Jeff, and I—and a host of mushing insiders—would consider it improbable and very difficult to win both races in the same year.

The reason is simple. The two races are more than 1,000 miles each, and the finish of the Yukon Quest is usually only ten days from the Iditarod start. What musher, even competing at the highest level, could steel him- or herself to the task of two consecutive wilderness treks in less than a month? Furthermore, how could a musher train two teams at a championship level? Surely one team of huskies could not win two back-to-back races of a thousand miles in arctic conditions.

That long-held belief has been blown to bits. On February 20, 2007, Lance and his team—including his redoubtable leaders Larry, Hobo, and Lippy—won his third consecutive Yukon Quest. The race was brutally cold, with temperatures as low as -55°F and rarely climbing above -10°F.

After a few days' rest, he loaded sixteen dogs, including twelve of his Yukon Quest huskies, and drove 350 miles to Anchorage for the start of the Iditarod on March 4, 2007. Lance was highly regarded, but few if any race pundits thought he had a chance of winning the Iditarod.

The competition was keen in 2007, with a host of Iditarod champions, including three who'd won it four times—Jeff King,

Martin Buser, and Doug Swingley. Also present was the two-time champ, Robert Sørlie of Norway; the 2004 champ, Mitch Seavey; and the five-time champ, a little older but still dangerous, Rick Swenson. A herd of top finishers was also set to make their mark in this extremely competitive field.

Out of this pack, Lance Mackey emerged in the last third of the race. He crossed the finish line and won the 2007 Iditarod on March 13, becoming the first musher to win both the Yukon Quest and the Iditarod in the same year—and he did it using the same dogs. Lance Mackey gained international recognition and in Alaska created a boisterous and enthusiastic fan club.

Of course, it was an unbelievable accomplishment. I interviewed Lance's father, Dick Mackey, in Nome that year. "I don't know if he realizes what he's just done," he said. "Nobody thought it was possible."

Sure, there were a few skeptics. Lance was given credit—somewhat reluctantly—and some held the view that it was just a lucky set of circumstances that allowed Lance to win both races. It would never happen again.

In 2008, Lance returned for his critics and, in a very deliberate way, made them eat their words. He won the Yukon Quest for the fourth time and the Iditarod for the second. Now it was really incredible.

A year later, Lance perfected his skills and won the 2009 Iditarod so convincingly that no one could doubt that he is one of the great mushers, not to mention an elite animal trainer. The Iditarod veterinarians were also impressed with his husbandry skills. Based on a series of rated factors, he was awarded the Humanitarian Award for best-conditioned animals in 2009.

So those are the statistics and numbers, the nuts-and-bolts parts of Lance Mackey. His fan base includes people from all around the world and in every age group, and when he's not training or racing, he's in demand for speaking engagements and appearances. Lance has appeared on *The Late Show with Conan O'Brien* and been featured on cable networks such as Discovery, Versus, and ESPN. In fact, two ESPY Award nominations from ESPN placed him among the country's greatest professional athletes following his 2007 and 2008 championships. Shortly afterward, he ranked second in *Sports Illustrated's* Toughest Athletes, followed by his designation as "World's Toughest Athlete," selected by Versus Channel viewers. And in 2009, Lance was inducted into the Alaska Sports Hall of Fame, referring to him as "one of the greatest mushers of all time."

The story of how he got there is the real subject of this book. I cannot disguise my admiration for Lance Mackey, and therefore it was an honor to work with him on this book about his life. I've had the privilege to watch Lance in action, but also to hear him contemplate his feelings about animals, especially his beloved sled dogs, family, and work. So I have a few observations of my own about the man and the musher.

Lance is at once a contradiction. Walk in the door at his house outside Fairbanks, Alaska, and you will be greeted by the chaos of his nine house pets: Ashley, Butter, Daphne, Chance, Jackey, Cleo, Monkey, Roman, and Pebbles (a little ball of gray fluff that fits in the crook of his arm). Add to this Joee, the loose roaming sled dog, and Trigger the cat. This pack includes a black and yellow Labrador, a Chihuahua, Pomeranian/Lhasa Apsos, and Jack Russells.

All seems madness, and yet it's well-organized. All the dogs are house broken, and as soon as Lance comes in the house they settle around him like the king's pack, while he says hello to each one. When I ask him about safety of the little Chihuahua or the Pomeranian that may venture into the sled-dog yard, he says, "The sled dogs respect these little guys. All these dogs are equally important to me."

This introduces me to an unusual side of Lance. He talks to each dog like he would to a child, and he takes the time through the day to eventually acknowledge all of them—including the seventy to one hundred in the sled-dog yard in front of the house. He also freely subscribes emotions and motives to each dog, as if he had each one professionally psychoanalyzed.

"This is a young two-year-old with a lot of pride," he says. "He may not be the most gifted athletically, but I want to give him the

Lance launched the Comeback Kennel in Kasilof, Alaska, and later moved to Fairbanks to train in tougher winter conditions. There are sixty to seventy dogs in the yard, and another dozen or so house pets. JON LITTLE PHOTO

honor of traveling with the team to Nome. I owe it to him. He knows that's how I feel, and that's why he's so dedicated to me." Sure enough, as he says this, the dog is on his hind legs, embraced by Lance, tail wagging. As we move about the dog yard, Lance tells me about each dog's personality, stage of personal development, and what his expectations are for his or her future. It's almost like he's running a career counseling center for sled dogs.

At the end of the tour, we say hello to Zorro, the foundation of Mackey's Comeback Kennel. Zorro, as you will learn, was severely injured in a snowmachine accident in 2008 that received nationwide media coverage. Zorro is like an old friend you've known since grade school. Lance says, "I put him here so I see him the first thing in the morning when I come to the dog yard, and I see him last when I walk into the house at the end of the day." Lance, a uniquely animated human, completes a complicated conversation with Zorro, and we head back into the house.

Sitting around the table with Lance is usually a brief event, because he's in perpetual motion. So you might assume that he's also irreversibly spontaneous in everything he does. But instead I discover another contradiction.

The man who seems the very example of a free spirit is actually incredibly organized. He and his wife, Tonya, also have an ability to identify a specific goal, apply a timetable and expectations to achieve that goal, and propose a budget to accomplish it. Of course, I should have known that, because that's characteristic of successful people.

This is not only a book about an Iditarod champ and a masterful animal trainer; it's an affirmation of the old adage, "Where the mind dares to go, the body will follow."

—JOE RUNYAN
1989 Iditarod Champion
1985 Yukon Quest Champion

CHAPTER 1 **A DREAM STATE**

Dreams do come true, Mama.

ust a few miles from the 2007 Iditarod finish line at Nome, I was studying my leader, Larry, a serious personality with a common gray coat, trotting on a trail ribboned with the fresh tracks of snowmachines. He was moving smoothly, with a steady purpose. We'd been together down this trail before in a mind-to-mind agreement to prove we were alive, not in a dream. Eight other dogs matched Larry's steady pace and leaned into the harness, bringing our 1,100-mile expedition closer to an end.

We followed the frozen beach, passing the occasional drift log that earlier this year may have traveled hundreds of miles down the Yukon River out to the Bering Sea. Just three weeks ago, we were upriver ourselves on another race, the 1,000-mile Yukon Quest International Sled Dog Race, on a route that followed the early gold-rush trails from Whitehorse, Canada, through the Klondike gold fields, and on to Fairbanks, Alaska. I'd traveled through unforgiving cold, down to -45°F, winding along the frozen Yukon River, through forests, and over mountains behind this same team of dogs. These stalwart athletes—I couldn't imagine a team with more honesty and dignity—had won the Yukon Quest for an incredible third time in a row. Ten days later, we loaded up the dog truck and headed south to Anchorage for the start of the Iditarod.

In less than a month, we set out on another grueling 1,100-mile race. But with each mile, the dogs gained more indestructible

Kicking to help the team as we approach Unalakleet in the 2007 race.
DONNA DEWHURST PHOTO

strength, and I experienced an invigorated state of being that numbed the physical inconveniences of cold and sleeplessness. Now we were closing in on the finish.

It seemed the entire village of Nome had come out to watch us enter this famous gold-strike town. Along the trail, clusters of villagers were bundled up in parkas and calling out as we passed, "Go, Lance!" "All right!" "Lance, you've done it!" I realized again that we were about to accomplish an "impossible" feat. Larry and the team had trotted and loped more than 2,000 miles in unrelenting cold, pulling over mountain ranges, knifing through wind, and earning a place in mushing history. I was honored to be with this team, and that they wanted to be with me on this journey.

My sled dogs are my passion and responsibility. I would rather be 10th than to be 1st with their spirit broken. But to win with a dog team that is trotting with such unstoppable power—like they could bore a hole through the earth—this was everything we'd trained for, hoped for.

There is always the comfort and beauty of watching my team trotting. Muscles on their hind legs, rhythmic, trotting with so much power. Effortless motion is what I see. Transfixed, I can stare for hours at my dogs moving across the white landscape, reminded that life itself is about moving forward—made authentic with risk. I'm willing to take risks to keep living, and my dogs are bold, always ready to share it with me. I've learned to force myself to look around, take my eyes off the team, even ride backward on my sled and look behind, to break the trance.

Now as we approached the finish line, I looked west, to where the Bering Sea, a limitless expanse of ice and open leads, was a pastel of blues and pinks with a setting sun. An unforgiving wind came out of the east and reminded us that we were vulnerable and miniscule on this treeless arctic landscape. I have this attitude now that life is temporary and time is measured.

The seed of my ambition to win the Quest and the Iditarod back-to-back was planted long before it bloomed with this dog team. Winning is an art form, a performance, a masterpiece that I wanted to present to the world. But first I had to conquer obstacles on my own hazardous trail.

I was born into the world of sled dogs—literally. My musher father was a cofounder of this very race, first launched in 1973; my musher mother was still running sprint races when she was seven months' pregnant with me. I grew up in the company of sled dogs, and sometimes I catch myself communicating with them like the little boy I was, alone in a yard of dogs while my single mom was at work and my dad had moved halfway across Alaska.

For years, I carried a chip on my shoulder. It began at age ten, when my parents divorced and, in some unexplainable way, I blamed myself. I was pissed off at the world, and I used my considerable energy to make a destructive impression. I made sure that no one in my path could forget the young Lance Mackey. And it worked.

I saw the disappointment in the eyes of my parents, noticed when a teacher shook her head in disbelief, watched a judge frown as he read my record, and numbed my vision with bouts of substance abuse and an indulged indifference.

It took me a while to climb over those obstacles, but I did it, and I don't have much sympathy for myself. That can make you cry, even more than physical pain.

Nome and the noise of civilization, with a helicopter and television camera overhead, was not far away when I decided to make an unscheduled stop. I have this habit, this commitment, to stop the team every two hours and feed them a snack. I'll grab my goodie bag, "Whoa" the team, and run to the front of the tandem line of my huskies. By the time I'm back to the sled, each one has had a rich sliver of food in less than a minute. This stop, however, was my opportunity to acknowledge each dog, each unique personality, put my hands on their heads and rub them down their backs. Two by two, they filled out that legend-making, durable team for this extraordinary year: Larry and Hobo, in the lead, followed by Foster, Lippy, Pauly, Boy Cuz, Fudge, Battel, and Handsome. At the end of the race, there would be little chance to really show my appreciation.

And we were off again. Larry and the front-end veterans of the team knew the way into Nome. They have a photographic memory of the trail and can speak to me through a mere hesitation in their pace. Now they were telling me, "The trail went that way, Boss, last year." To ease their concern, I called out, "On by, it's okay, Larry," letting him and his front-end mates know that I understood the confusion. As we passed the far side of a drift log, I chuckled to myself that Larry was right. The trail was on the other side last time.

Larry is a leader like none other. He's become so popular that fans join the "Larry Appreciation Society" and sew a patch on their clothes.

From the sea ice, I could distinctly see the buildings of Nome, a lone, remote outpost on the Bering Sea Coast. The team was in that perfect dance where all nine dogs, magnificent animals, moved my magic sled closer to the finish.

The experience, approaching Nome, was deeply emotional. Tears began to flow in the privacy of my moving band of sled dogs, for reasons greater than earning first place.

Six years earlier, I'd been holding on with all of my strength just to cross the finish line of the Iditarod. When the team pulled to a stop, pain had buckled my knees, and I'd collapsed into my wife's arms. "Babe, I need to go to the hospital," I'd whispered. Within days we learned, although we already knew, that it was much more than extreme fatigue. I had a malignant tumor in my neck. The big "C." The weeks and months that followed were filled with surgeries, radiation, pain meds, rehab . . . and determination to get back on a sled. I learned from cancer that I could overcome physical deficiencies with mental toughness. Pain, and the risk that comes with it, is only relative to what you're willing to accomplish.

All those thoughts and memories, good and bad, dissolved as Larry and the team surged up the slip and off the beach to Front Street, Nome. My silent reverie was over, and my head was filled with the chants of a crowd who wanted to share this historic accomplishment with me and the team. The pain in my hands and feet, ever with me since the radiation treatments, moved to the back of my mind as we trotted the last four city blocks to the finish.

Running next to the sled down Front Street, I saw this victory as my artistic creation, my passion realized, a gift to my wife, my

I broke away from the media and crowd to hug my mother and we shared a quiet moment together. JEFF SCHULTZ /ALASKASTOCK

parents, family and fans. I viewed my dog team as a sculpture, alive and unbelievable, and I knew this team would be long remembered.

We entered a scene of chaotic celebration as we slipped under the carved log structure known as the "Burled Arch," etched with those welcome words: *End of Iditarod Sled Dog Race.* I was mugged, hugged, and overwhelmed. But I stole the chance, in a little moment of silence, to lean over my mother, the woman I'd put through hell for many a year and who'd stood by me for many a year. I hugged her tight and whispered, "Dreams do come true, Mama."

My face wet with tears, I turned back to the microphones and cameras and the glory of watching a wreath of yellow roses go around Larry's neck. I kissed my wife and punched the air. I would hold this scene in my head for the rest of my days.

This life of mine. It really is a dream.

CHAPTER 2 **BORN TO MUSH**

My father helped prove the skeptics wrong.

he first ten years of my life were spent in a world regulated by the noise and activity of the mushing world. My mother reminds me that this is truer than I could imagine. Incredibly, she was seven months' pregnant with me in March of 1970 when she placed 4th in the Women's North American Championships, held in Fairbanks.

The race was a three-day event of 10 miles on day one, 10 miles on day two, and a final third-day stage of 14 miles. In sprint racing, the dogs surge to speeds of well over 25 mph and easily lope at 16 to 20 mph on the trail. I now know that it takes skill, a learned confidence in the dogs, and real athleticism to negotiate the sharp curves and keep the sled on the trail. That was Mom, then known as Kathie Mackey.

And that was a great ride for an unborn baby. Maybe I sensed the run and it imprinted on me somehow, a claim my mother still makes. Even now, I always enjoy watching a sprint race, with the mushers taking deep, nervous breaths and doing knee bends at the start line to limber up for a thrill that is as good as any carnival ride. Asked about her accomplishment now, Mom just shrugs and says, "No big deal."

Following the 1969–70 race season, as Alaskans enjoyed the sun-drenched days leading up to Solstice, I was born on June 2. Family photos show that by that fall, I was tucked into a baby basket and set outside on the snow, while my parents prepared for a sprint race.

As far as I was concerned, my early childhood was paradise, secure

7

ABOVE LEFT: *When your mother is a sprint racer, a dogsled is your baby carriage. Here I am at four months old.* RIGHT: *I cut loose for a run during a family visit to Mount McKinley National Park, as Denali National Park was still known in the early 1970s.*

and action-filled. I lived with my parents and my younger brother Jason in a nice home, a double-wide trailer with some additions—including an office for my father—in Wasilla, Alaska. I knew about my half-brothers, Rick and Bill, and half-sister Becky from Dad's first marriage, but we never lived together. Later they and my other half- and step-siblings—Wesley, Chris, Kay, Kristin, and Kim—would become an important part of my extended family.

While other kids may have grown up with lawns and gardens outside their homes, outside ours was a sprawling dog yard—home to my parents' race team. Sled dogs greeted me every time I stepped out the door. Wrestling with the pups, a free-for-all mauling for boy and dogs, is one of my earliest memories. Huskies erupting into a frenzy of barking at feeding time, the squeals and screams, the mad yodeling of dogs harnessed for a training run, and the late-night howls, the sled dogs almost sounding like wolves in the cold, were all part of my daily experience.

By age five, I was already mushing dogs, and totally confident at it. I may have only been driving one, two, three, or four dogs, but I had ways for convincing a sixty-pound sled dog—much bigger than I was—to pull me down the trail.

I've always had the idea that a sled dog could run like hell, pull hard, and go fast for a long time. As a child, I also understood that each sled dog had a unique personality, and they responded, just like people, to praise, kindness, and respect. Years later, I still think of my dogs as my babies, and in many ways, I haven't changed how I communicate with them—just as I did as a boy. More recently, I realized that what I think is obvious about a dog's personality or behavior may really be a unique skill or insight I picked up as child.

I was three years old in 1973 when the first Iditarod Trail Sled Dog Race was born. A race from Anchorage to Nome was a major departure from the traditional sprint-racing format that was then popular in Alaska's villages and at the tracks in Anchorage and Fairbanks. In fact, ripping along on a groomed trail was what got my parents hooked on sled dogs in the beginning.

But instead of an all-out display of speed for 10 to 30 miles, the Iditarod was a new idea. This long-distance race would test men and women and their dogs over many days and miles. It was a return to the mentality of the Klondike days when toughened gold miners transported freight to their remote claims with the husky. The mushers on the 1973 Iditarod were pioneers of the 1,100-mile race trail, snowshoeing along old trails that had once led to the gold fields—including the strike on the Iditarod River in southwestern Alaska. The town that boomed there in the early twentieth century is now a ghost town and a checkpoint on the race in alternating years.

My father Dick Mackey was part of that first history-making group of mushers who decided to try the unknown and mush from Anchorage to Nome. Back then, some considered those early race organizers dreamers, ultimate adventurers, or fools. Diehard critics and even some doubting mushers thought the 1,100-mile course an impossibility, outside the capabilities of a sled dog. But they were proven wrong. That first race, the monumental effort to relive the history of Alaska, was won by Dick Wilmarth from Red Devil, Alaska, in a time of 20 days, 49 minutes, and 41 seconds.

My father helped prove the skeptics wrong, too. He finished 7th in that first Iditarod, after 22 days and 4 hours on the trail. With a well-established and marked trail, mushers in my era can do it in half the time—fewer than ten days. That tells me that those first mushers had to really work to bust out trails. They were in the bottom of the learning curve and just figuring out how to feed and care for dogs while traveling long-distance. They also tested themselves and learned to function for days in the arctic winter.

Dad may have been a dedicated sprint-racing enthusiast, but all that changed dramatically with his new fascination: the Iditarod. He's always been a social person, and typically his friends would beat a path to our house for coffee and endless talk about dogs and the Iditarod. I was a kid with a lot of energy, so I was running around the house at Mach 1 while the stream of mushers came and went from our table. Of course, Dad is also a restless guy, so he probably thought it was normal to have a kid bouncing off the walls while he entertained friends.

What I remember most is meeting the legends of my sport: Joe Redington, Sr., one of the most determined founders of the Iditarod and a tireless promoter; Dick Tozier, who often took the job of Iditarod Race Marshal in the early years; Dave Olson, a musher and one of the men who made improvements to the overgrown trail. These friends and many others were caught up in the adventure of the Iditarod.

Larry "Cowboy" Smith was another character who dropped by the house to stay before Iditarod. He never won the Iditarod but he was famous for being the "rabbit," often taking a big lead in the first part of the race, never afraid to go out ahead and break trail. He always created a lot of excitement in the press and was a consistent contender, in fact, finishing 3rd when my older brother Rick Mackey won the 1983 Iditarod. Larry was from Dawson in Canada's Yukon, where they had a tradition of running bigger dogs on the trap-lines.

"Cowboy" Smith was a fascinating visitor for a small boy—a real outdoorsman. He did all kinds of things in the wilderness—trapping, running a barge, big-game guiding—but one of his more interesting activities was horses and rodeo. He wore a big, black cowboy hat, something we didn't see except on television. I also haven't forgotten his dogs. They were huge, steady-traveling work dogs—some of them in the eighty-pound range. For a little kid, it was thrilling to go outside and see Larry's team of huskies.

Visiting our home, each one of the mushers made an impression on me. Conversations around the table went on at all times of the day and late at night. I might not remember their exact words, but I knew who they were and that they were talking sled dogs. Today these mushers are older, and some have passed on, but they remain my boyhood heroes of mushing. As an adult, I've enjoyed watching them pursue their own dreams.

AROUND OUR PLACE, there was always some kind of activity related to the dogs. As part of a normal day, buckets of thawing meat and bags of dry commercial feed were arranged on the floor for mixing the dogs' rations, while a special snack for the dogs—liver—was cooking on the stove.

Mom was always busy either making or fixing racing gear. She never stopped sewing booties for the dogs—and I mean by the thousands. In a bad snow year, when the snow balls up between the dogs' toes, it's absolutely necessary to put cloth boots on their paws to protect the soft tissue from rub spots. In long-distance sled dogs, you could be faced with small splits in the soft tissue between the toes, or even worse, the splits could become infected. If that happens, you have a dog that's out of the race.

These days, it's not uncommon for a conscientious musher to boot dogs the entire 1,100 miles to Nome, and to change boots twice a day. The number of booties necessary for racing and training could add up to thousands. You can buy them now, but back then, Mom made them all.

My father's focus—obsession, really—was the Iditarod. He kept after the race year after year, always finishing in the Top 10, until he finally won it on his sixth try in 1978, crossing the finish line after 14 days, 18 hours, 52 minutes, and 24 seconds. I mention seconds because the 1978 Iditarod was an unforgettable, epic battle between Dick Mackey and Rick Swenson that landed in the record books.

Swenson was a young, opinionated, and openly confident musher who'd already won the 1977 Iditarod at age twenty-six. The media favorite, Swenson was the younger man, and was known to occasionally talk some trash. My Dad enjoyed the challenge and planned on doing battle. He was forty-six years old, but he'd spent plenty of time with some rough guys as an Alaskan ironworker, and had the mental toughness to race and play the psych game with anybody. The two were locked together for days, in and out of checkpoints and rarely losing sight of each other. It was Dad's intention to shadow Swenson all the way to Nome, and he was going to have a shot at winning. Their race would go down as the closest finish in Iditarod history.

Although I've learned the details over the years, I hold crystal-clear images from a child's point of view. I remember waiting in a room with my mother and some Iditarod personnel who were keeping track of the two leaders as they approached Nome. It seemed like we waited there forever along with a big crowd of fans.

I was standing close to Mom, looking up at her through an eight-year-old's eyes. As people came by and talked about the race—that it was a close one, that Dad had a good chance of winning—I remember Mom smiling. She even had tears in her eyes. I sensed the excitement, but I had no idea of how important this was or how much work my parents had invested in this race.

As people crowded in and the press sought to interview my mother, I was shoved around, but I just held onto her until someone said it was time to move out on Front Street. Everybody knew that Mackey and Swenson had pushed for days. Everybody knew they were about to witness the final efforts of two exhausted competitors. The crowd piled through the doors, and we waited with the press behind the Burled Arch (the traditional marker for the finish line, constructed from burled spruce logs and spanning the street).

As we waited, people kept leaning over and asking me what I thought about the prospect of my Daddy winning the race. I really didn't know what to say. And for sure, I didn't fully understand what it meant to win the Iditarod—but I was paying attention.

In those days, communication was not sophisticated; however, in the checkpoints, volunteer ham radio operators were feeding the world tantalizing accounts of the mushers as they checked in and out, so we knew the two men were traveling in tandem. Word was they were out of Safety, the closest checkpoint to Nome, just 18 miles south on the coast.

The Bering Sea Coast is constantly hammered by storms, and you can usually count on a cold, stiff wind. This is a land famous for the one-piece pullover Eskimo parka trimmed with wolf ruff, the favored survival gear for mushers. Riding behind the sled in a storm requires a good parka, or your life could be in jeopardy. But no matter how cold it gets, life inside a good parka can be almost tropical, especially if you're running hard on a race to the finish.

My father couldn't take off his Eskimo parka because at the Safety checkpoint, race officials had tightly tied a race bib over it, effectively pinning him inside. The numbered bib helps identify mushers as the teams approach the final miles, but that year, there were a few kinks in the idea. He was running, sweating and damn near suffocating from heat inside his parka. But if he stopped to strip the bib off, he'd lose a shot at winning the race of his life.

When the crowd spotted the two men moving up Front Street in a virtual tie, they went crazy. From the Arch, I could see my father running toward us, and the noise all around as Mom and the rest of the crowd were screaming and yelling. I saw Swenson running next to his sled, so close to Dad. Suddenly, when they were almost on top of us, we were pushed aside to make room for the arriving dog teams.

In the final, heated moments of the race, with the crowd in a frenzy of cheers, my father came into the finish chute. At the moment his lead dog crossed the finish line, he collapsed beside his sled, gasping for air, sweat just pouring off his head, the only part of his body exposed to the cold air. Though he was straddling the finish line, with his lead dog across the line and his sled just short of it, Dad was convinced that he'd won.

A blink later, Swenson's lead dog crossed the line, and he then passed his rival and got his entire sled over the line.

My Mom and brother and I looked at Dad collapsed on the ground. All we wanted to do was to get closer and give him a hug—but nobody would let us. I kept looking at him and asking, "What's wrong with Dad? Why can't he walk?"

"He's all right!" Mom yelled over all the noise. "He'll be okay!"

A great debate had broken out. Everybody was shouting, "Who won?!"—even the officials. One of them declared Swenson the winner, but the others called a halt. They decided to make a phone call to review the finish with Dick Tozier, who normally marshaled the race, but was out sick in Anchorage. One of the co-marshals, Myron Gavin, would later be quoted again and again after he pronounced, "They don't take a picture of the horse's ass, do they?"

The final ruling: Dick Mackey had won the closest race in Iditarod history by one second. The younger Swenson, who would become a dominating Iditarod champion, congratulated him. Through the years, Swenson would win a record five Iditarods and compete in a record-breaking thirty Iditarods.

That victory for Dad was a huge event at our house. He'd trained a champion dog team, executed a good strategy, but most importantly, he'd played a psych game with Rick Swenson for miles and never allowed himself to deviate from his goal: to win.

Reliving the images and emotions of that finish is easy for me. It burns a permanent feeling into your heart when you see your father collapse from an extraordinary effort. I believe that experience has a lot to do with my own drive and devotion to the sport. Had Dad not been successful, or had I not been there to watch that finish, it's hard to say if I would have the passion that drives me now.

My father's 1978 win over Rick Swenson was one for the record books.
ROB STAPLETON / ALASKASTOCK

Back at home, Dad would spend most of his winters training sled dogs, but in the summers he traveled the state, moving from job to job as an ironworker. Because he was always on the move, training and racing the dogs or working, my brother and I were essentially raised by our mother. We admired Dad, but he was a moving target—just checking in at home and then leaving again—and we really didn't know him.

Dick Mackey lived, breathed, and dreamed about the Iditarod during my early years. As a result, I think it's fair to say that he didn't dedicate large amounts of time to his family and in my particular case—to me. He was passionate about launching the Iditarod and single-minded about winning it. Now I can understand the juggling it takes to balance family and a passion like dog mushing.

Nevertheless, I remember my first ten years as predictable. In my world, I was secure, accustomed to the rhythm of my parents' lives, the constant flow of visitors, and the daily routine of the sled dogs.

For the first ten years, the winds were gentle. And then my parents divorced, a marker in my life that still defines me. This was an

Before and after my parents divorced, I found comfort and purpose with the dogs. Here I am showing off my first trophy for the Aurora Junior 50, with my leader, Stevie. We took 2nd place.

earthquake, chaos and destruction, downpours and lightning, wind and snow, flooding, hurricane, tornado, every word you could use to describe a young boy's life that's abruptly changed, turned upside down and inside out. I was lost in the storm. I went through the range of emotions, from being angry, wanting attention, and feeling abandoned, to completely baffled. It was a tough time, but I realize now that it prepared me for my own storms that still lay ahead.

CHAPTER 3 **WILD CHILD**

. . . getting into trouble was easy with absolutely no guidance.

he house that once had been a center of constant visitor traffic was now sadly quiet and conspicuously vacant. The dog yard, once populated by some of the best long-distance dogs in the world, was now home to a few remnants that occasionally broke the quiet with short bouts of aimless barking. The wild exuberance and unrestrained energy of the race team, and the fast-moving musher who'd won the Iditarod, were gone from my life.

Jason and I just couldn't figure out what we'd done to deserve this. In some unexplained way, I thought I was responsible. It was a huge emotional blow for a ten-year-old, and I couldn't talk about it. Actions, some of them not coherent even for a youngster, became my main means of expression.

Dad had left behind about a dozen dogs, I guess to keep our minds off the divorce and maybe to give us a little responsibility and sense of direction. They were leftovers—scrap dogs—but good enough to get us down the trail. Looking back on it, that was fine. We were ready to roll with that. We were just kids, so any kind of planning for the future, like racing the Iditarod or sled dogs as a passion, was just way beyond our ability to think about clearly.

Then and now, my mother was a hard worker and very practical. She never finished high school, but that never stopped her from making a living. Mom always maintained that hard work could overcome any obstacle. She told me and Jason that if we worked hard to take care of the dogs, she would make sure they were provided with dog food and equipment. When I grew up, she told me that she worked so hard because she felt the sled dogs were a sort of birthright that she wanted to give to her sons. It was an extra budget item, but she always managed.

I was already immersed in the world of sled dogs, so it was natural to think about running the Junior Iditarod as a goal. The race was first staged in 1978 as a learning experience for younger mushers from fourteen to seventeen years old. The race is held on the weekend before the Iditarod—which starts on the first Saturday of March—and basically follows a part of the Iditarod Trail in a 160-mile loop from either Knik or Willow to Skwentna and back. Over the years it's developed into a good two-day competition with a lot of benefits, including some prizes, and helps build friendships with other junior mushers.

While it seemed logical to set our hearts on eventually running the Junior Iditarod, money was tight and Mom was working two jobs just to keep up. Jason and I were in school during the day, but we got home early enough to hook up a team of sled dogs. While Mom was still at work, my brother and I would harness the dogs, get a sled and tow line organized, and head out for what we thought was a long run. We'd often go for a 25- or 30-mile run, feel like we were gone forever, and get home in the dark.

These days, when I'm talking about my childhood with friends, especially those who've grown up in a more stable situation, they're amazed that two little boys would come home and harness up a team for a 30-mile training run. There wasn't anybody to tell us to put on warm clothes, or to help us decide about gear, or where we were going to go. We did that all on our own. No one led us out of the dog yard. It was just between us and the dogs. My mother figured we were smart enough to put on a pair of mitts if our hands got cold. Plus, we did the chores—fed the dogs, cleaned up the dog lot, and then went inside and did some more chores that she'd asked us to do. She made us self-reliant.

We were busy, but we were also genuinely pissed off at the world—especially me. At ten, I was the oldest man in the house. I was mad at my father, who'd moved on and was with his new wife. And although I may not have thought about it consciously, I was probably teed off at Mom, too. I didn't like what was happening at home. I didn't understand it at all.

In 1981, my father started a new business above the Arctic Circle along a gravel road that was built for construction access during the building of the Trans-Alaska Pipeline. Known as the Haul Road, the crude highway's official name is the Dalton Highway. Dad had settled near an old gold-rush town named Wiseman and close to a former pipeline construction camp known as Coldfoot. The place is about halfway between Fairbanks and the Prudhoe Bay oilfields on the edge of the Arctic Ocean. From Fairbanks, Coldfoot is about 260 miles. But from where we lived at Big Lake, getting to Dad's was a long 575 miles one way. And they didn't call it Coldfoot just for fun, either. It's one of the coldest places in Alaska, with winter temperatures regularly dropping to -50°F or -60°F.

At that time, truckers constantly ran up the Haul Road to its dead-end at the Prudhoe Bay oilfields, then back again. Dad's idea was to sell food and fix flats. Typical of my father, he started the business just toughing it out, living in a couple of army surplus tents and selling coffee and hamburgers out of an old school bus on the side of the gravel road. But he had good business sense. At the height of the traffic, a truck a minute would come through Coldfoot.

Everybody knew Dad as an Iditarod champ, and they all liked him. He worked hard, and he was innovative. From the truckers hauling loads to Prudhoe, he hustled plywood that had been used for containers of insulation. He bought materials and salvage from some of the pipeline camps, and he eventually put together a restaurant and shop in a remote and brutally cold location. In a few short years, it became a successful business and a routine halfway stop for Haul Road truckers. Later, he sold it at a good profit to a tour operator, and it now provides accommodations for visitors to the North Slope.

Three Mackey brothers fishing with our little cousin, Brenda. I'm on the left, then Jason, and Rick. DICK AND CATHY MACKEY COLLECTION

Jason and I began spending the summers with Dad at Coldfoot and winters with Mom at Big Lake, happily back among our sled dogs. It was such a long way to travel between Coldfoot and Big Lake that our life was never continuous with our parents. It was just one or the other.

I was fourteen when I finally found myself at the Junior Iditarod start line for my first race. Jason and I had already been training for years. In many ways, I was looking for approval from my parents as much as wanting to compete. Of course, Dad placed importance on doing well, and my older brother Rick had made his mark by winning the Iditarod in 1983, making Dick and Rick Mackey the only father-son to win the Iditarod.

Putting together a good dog team was important to me and Jason, so we'd been hustling deals with neighbors or friends to borrow good dogs for our team. We also tried every dog that was available—sometimes it was a smorgasbord of just plain crap dogs—but we weren't afraid to get out and look, especially if the price was in our range, which was zero.

Eventually, I got to the start line with a fair team of dogs for my first Junior Iditarod. Rick helped me out with a couple of dogs, including a good leader named Joker, who I will never forget.

Day one of the race marked the first time I'd ever been really out in the woods alone and in unfamiliar country. I thought I was out in the middle of nowhere and was completely turned around when I finally arrived at Yentna Station, the first checkpoint for the real Iditarod. Things worked out all right, and I finished 10th that day. By the end of the race on the day two, however, I felt a real sense of accomplishment, just by finishing. I started looking forward to the next year.

We learned a lot, so our feeding and training strategy improved for the following year. By then, we were a little more disciplined and had added many more training miles to our schedule. The quality of the dog team didn't really change, but my approach did, and we finished 6th in Junior Iditarod on attempt number two. As the oldest brother, I had pick of the dog yard, but that didn't stop Jason. We were inseparable as brothers, but we were also competitive. Jason actually beat me, taking 5th that year with the second team, and taught me

Having fun in the Junior Iditarod. It seemed that dog of mine, Ribbit, was always in the sled.

Running the Junior World Championship Sled Dog Race.

that management by the musher, not just the quality of the dogs, gets you to the finish first.

Jason and I had reason to be proud, since we were the ones who did all the work of putting the team together. Some of the other junior mushers had the advantage of ready-made teams from their parents' kennels and lots of expert advice and help. Some of them literally just jumped on the runners behind a really well-trained dog team and went for a ride on race day.

My mother, as always, never stopped working hard at two jobs. We continued to come home from school, knock out the standard chores of washing dishes and taking out the garbage, and then change our clothes for work in the dog yard. At that time, we had a traditional dog-food cooker—the pot was the bottom half of a fifty-five-gallon fuel drum, and the cooker was the top half of the drum. We'd gather wood, get a fire  going, haul buckets of water to the dog pot, and cook salmon or meat. We hustled dog food anywhere we could find it—getting extra fish,

cleaning out people's freezers in the spring, picking up road kills, whatever it took to put something in the dog pot. Then we would throw in some rice or maybe some cheap commercial dog food to thicken the stew—and that's what we fed to the dogs. And as fast as we could get things done, we'd hook up ten dogs and go for a 30-mile training run.

Jason and I never suffered from too much expert advice. Mom and Dad were still pretty much at odds with each other, and Dad was still nearly 600 miles north. We did talk occasionally, but it was always about other subjects than dogs.

Good or bad, my unsupervised experience with sled dogs as a young kid probably made me think about and understand them in a unique way. By necessity, I was already forced to figure out what motivated a sled dog to haul my butt down the trail. I think it helps me now to try to figure out how they're looking at the world.

By age fourteen, I was also devoting serious energy to developing my rebellious behavior. I had a chip on my shoulder. School was becoming a real distraction to my main activity—which was getting into trouble. My mother said school was important, and I might have actually believed it to a certain point, but getting into trouble was easy with absolutely no guidance. To me, school was nothing more than a full-time babysitter. Jason and I were kids gone wild in an environment where a lot of things and a lot of people could easily influence active kids like us. I have to admit that I was the main culprit for trouble. I just sucked my brother into the mix. Jason and I did see a lot of things and a side of life that we don't want our own kids to experience.

Gradually, hanging out with my friends and doing whatever the hell I wanted to do became more important than school, and eventually more important than the dogs. I couldn't wait for the weekends, so I could go to the latest party and find more trouble.

Even the simplest instructions from my mother became an exercise in rebellion. If she said, "Be home by midnight," I would make sure I waited a block or two from the house, even if I was on time, to be an hour late. The hour might have given me time to think about another act of destruction for the next day.

When I was fifteen, we moved to Petersburg, a major commercial fishing port in southeastern Alaska. My mother had her pilot's license and had just gotten a job flying patrols with the Alaska Department of Fish and Game. We weren't there two days, and I decided to take an unannounced expedition by skiff to Wrangell with this guy I'd just met. This was the first time I'd ever been on the ocean, much less had any experience with boating or tides. Eventually, my mother found

A successful salmon fisherman in 1984.

out where I was and tracked me down by telephone in Wrangell. She advised me it was a high tide, so that we could get back through the Wrangell Narrows, and I needed to get my butt back to Petersburg.

We left Wrangell, but when we didn't show up for days, Mom was frantic, flying the beaches looking for us, holding her breath every time she saw bald eagles feeding on a carcass, figuring that her oldest son was the main course. We had run out of gas, and eventually made it back after three days. Naturally, I didn't care at the time that I'd inconvenienced anybody, including my mother. Sure, she read me the riot act, but it didn't change my attitude.

More parenting adventures were ahead for my poor Mom. Back in Wasilla, she let us borrow her new truck while she took another vehicle to work. And Jason and I got into an accident. We staged it pretty well, but she must have been suspicious when we ran out the driveway as she drove in from work. "Mom, you wouldn't believe it! We just went down to the 7-Eleven, and some guy creamed us in the parking lot!"

The longer she looked at the truck, the more convinced she was that a parking lot accident probably did not happen. It must have been really tough for her. Only recently has she discovered the truth behind many similar incidents. She maintains that I was making a serious effort to put her in API, the Alaska Psychiatric Institute.

In total, I was a dedicated behavior problem. I had even lost interest in the sled dogs. As a result, the dogs became a burden to me, my brother, and my mother, who was still working to pay for their food and maintenance. By the time I was sixteen, our sled dogs were slowly being given away or sold.

Some of them were farmed out to Lolly Medley, who was a knowledgeable musher, a really fine harness-maker, and an Iditarod finisher in 1974, the race's second year. Women run the Iditarod all the time now, but in the early years it was unusual for a woman to compete in the race. It took her nearly twenty-nine days, but she was one of two women to finish that year.

Lolly was kind-hearted, and I was just plain irresponsible. Originally, the deal was the dogs were just supposed to camp at her place while I supplied the dog food. Over time, I stopped dropping off dog food, and gradually—out of sight, out of mind—I forgot about the dogs. Lolly has since passed away, but I haven't forgotten her understanding and gentle personality. For all I know, her sons Cim and Ramey Smyth, both of whom regularly place among the Top 10 Iditarod finishers, could be using some of the old bloodlines from those dogs.

At sixteen, my enthusiasm for the dogs was replaced by a mindless cycle of partying and causing trouble, a lot of it destructive. My parents were ready to do something about their problem child.

CHAPTER 4 **THE COLDFOOT 'SOLUTION'**

. . . it was understandable that my behavior puzzled many people.

n my view of the world, anything I did as a teen-ager was all about figuring it out, because nothing was handed to me. I just had to work my ass off for everything I received.

When I did get my first car, it wasn't because somebody in the family thought it would be a nice way for "little" Lance to get back and forth to school, or as a reward for getting good grades. For me, that first car was all about wheeling and dealing, and doing everything I could to get something I felt I needed.

My final years in high school were turbulent and definitely not focused on academics. I was ready to move on. I was getting into some more serious trouble, and it was obvious that my mother had lost what little control she'd once had. My parents decided to send me up to Coldfoot, which had grown from tents and an old bus into a growing truck stop with a restaurant, fuel sales, and repair shop.

Deciding on my move must have seemed logical to my parents, but it had certain elements of a rush decision to me. It was late October, the days were short, and the nights long and dark. We were already well into winter in Alaska. My mother came home from work at 10:30 P.M. and told me, "Pack your bag, Lance. We're driving to Coldfoot." She'd reached her limit.

Years later, Mom told me that she was holding her breath in that moment. Her greatest fear was that I would say, "No." That would have left her completely out of options and powerless to direct me

My father and I are on the right in this line-up, with the crew who helped build the café at Coldfoot in 1982. Dick Mackey Collection

The truck stop at Coldfoot became an overnight stopping point for tourists traveling up the Haul Road. My father had built the Arctic Acres Inn by renovating camp trailers that had been used in the building of the Trans-Alaska Pipeline. Tricia Brown photo

in any way. Fortunately, I packed my things, Mom drove through the long night, and I moved up to Dad's place at Coldfoot.

The theory was that since Coldfoot, above the Arctic Circle, remote and isolated—which it was—was 575 miles removed from all my friends—which it was—and that Dad was a better candidate to control me. All of it had some element of truth. To them, it seemed like a pretty good strategy for getting me straightened out.

Unfortunately, Dad was also running a big business with lots of employees and projects that needed finishing. The weather could be miserably bum with snow or extremely cold temperatures—some of the coldest recorded in Alaska—and it was a constant battle to keep everything running. The summer was a little easier, but it didn't last long. Big tractor-trailers, loaded to the maximum with pipe, equipment, and supplies for the North Slope oilfields, were pulling into Coldfoot one after the other, and the action never stopped twenty-four hours a day. One wall of the Coldfoot restaurant was covered with hundreds of coffee cups, each belonging to a long-haul truck driver.

Dad was hustling and just did not have time to devote time to the family or to really keep track of me, which was okay by me. I stayed on through the summer at Coldfoot and turned seventeen. I had some responsibilities—washing dishes, changing tires, and working a lot of hours. I also got to spend some time with a man who I really didn't know very well.

My father's autobiography, *One Second to Glory*, is a good read for anyone who wants to understand why people do wild things in Alaska. It also helped me understand my own childhood. In hindsight, I was lucky that he was a dog musher and a wild and energetic Alaskan. Now in his seventies, he's still a tough guy, very competitive and focused. He's mellowed over the years, but back then he used to say, "You ain't nothing as a musher unless you win the Iditarod." That sticks in your mind, even if you know it isn't true.

Initially, living in Coldfoot was good for me, but gradually the time I got with Dad was less and less. I started feeling more like an

At Coldfoot, I helped my brother Rick get his food drop bags ready for the 1987 Iditarod. The checkpoint names are preprinted on the outside of the bags.
DICK AND CATHY MACKEY COLLECTION

A little older and more experienced, I finish another Junior Iditarod.
DICK AND CATHY MACKEY COLLECTION

Dad and I may look like we're laying down on the job, but that was actually the mass start position for the 1986 Coldfoot Classic. Rules required the musher to start from the sleeping bag, jump up, and go.
DICK AND CATHY MACKEY COLLECTION

employee and less like a son. To get attention from my Dad, I started pulling stupid stunts that were more than he anticipated.

Across the Haul Road from the truck stop was a dirt-strip airport with electrical orange cones on each side of the runway lined up so pilots could see where to land. The landing strip was important to the small community at Wiseman and Coldfoot, because that's how people move around in the Bush. That's also how we got any deliveries for emergency parts, mail, and medivacs. The cones along the airstrip were especially important in winter with limited, subdued daylight.

I decided it would be a good idea to take Dad's truck and use all my skills and intelligence to run over all those orange cones. It was a well-executed plan, and I managed to totally, efficiently destroy all the cones—for no reason—and basically shut down the airstrip. I didn't care about the consequences. Of course, it was ridiculous and stupid, but I did get ten minutes of Dad's time. He also chewed me out in front of the local police officer, and I got to know the both of them a little better.

To this day, I really don't know why I was so destructive. I didn't hurt anybody directly, but I damaged a lot of things. It didn't look like much had changed in my life. Dad was extremely disappointed, and burned into my memory are images of the frustration on his face as he looked at me. For a long time, I struggled to gain his approval, but my methods were not successful. Of course, it was understandable that my behavior puzzled many people.

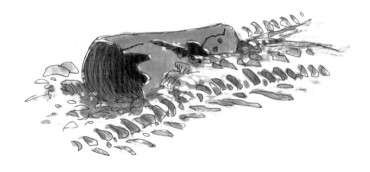

My life at Coldfoot had turned into just working and hanging around with other employees. A lot of my co-workers—and many truckers who passed through Coldfoot—weren't the greatest role models. Drugs and alcohol were always part of the social life there. You could get and experiment with anything you wanted above the Arctic Circle.

I was almost eighteen, working lots of hours, and making good money working at Coldfoot. Meanwhile, my mother, who really thought she'd done the right thing sending me up north, believed that I was improving and was working on my school work for high school on the Alaska home-school program. None of that was happening. In reality, I was getting worse.

Dad's business sense and hard work was paying off, and he was putting Coldfoot on the map. He started thinking about selling the place, especially when Princess Tours became interested. The huge tour operator had an eye toward moving clients up the Haul Road to tour the North Slope oilfields. Princess was going to experiment that summer by running tourists through Coldfoot, so Dad asked if I would stay the season and work as a luggage handler. I was starting to get my own ideas, and no, I didn't want any part of it.

It was time to get the hell out of Dodge and disconnect from my parents.

CHAPTER 5 **FROM THE ARCTIC CIRCLE TO THE HIGH SEAS**

If all else fails, I can work hard.

'd earned some money at Dad's place, but when I left Coldfoot, my only real possession was a new accumulation of ten dogs of my own. It seemed I had this easy way of gathering up dogs—then again, I was also in a family where collecting sled dogs was normal.

With no real destination other than my mother's place, I was going nowhere with a pack of sled dogs that I couldn't afford to feed. Of course, Mom was happy to see me, but I was old enough to realize that "Return of Lance" was a broken record. Back home for longer than I had planned, I thought about going back to school, but my mother had her own set of house rules and her own life, which led to the occasional collision.

That's when I recalled that Martin Buser, a local musher who'd once offered me a job. I was barely a teen-ager when I'd first met Martin, while he was racing the Tustumena 200 on the Kenai Peninsula, south of Anchorage. I was actually a good choice, truthfully, because I was a hard worker and motivated around dogs. So I called him up, and I'll be darned, he said he would hire me. I explained that I had this "little housing problem" for ten sled dogs. To Martin's credit, he rolled dog maintenance of my team into our agreement.

Working with Martin was a good experience. This was 1988—before he went on to win four Iditarods—1992, 1994, 1997, and 2002—and make his mark on the mushing world. He was full of energy and fun, and his Swiss heritage gave him an attention to detail and organization. I had a lot of energy, too, and a few ideas, and an ambition of my own that occasionally ran counter to Martin's training outlook.

My job was just basic kennel help—anything that needed to be done, like keeping the place tidy, feeding the dogs, helping Martin harness and hook-up for training runs—all those many jobs done every day at a big, seventy-dog kennel.

Martin was good with me, despite my own interpretation of sled dogs. I was there in the early fall, so we were training the dogs pulling a four-wheeler ATV on dirt trails instead of running a sled on snow. I had plenty of opinions to offer, especially since my father was already an Iditarod champ, and my brother Rick was an Iditarod champ and still winning races. In my mind, naturally I had some good ideas.

Martin would counter, "Well, I have a few different ideas that I want to try at my kennel." As it turned out, of course you can win with different styles.

Unfortunately, I also took advantage of Martin's good will and brought in a few more dogs above the agreed ten-dog limit. My brother Jason had a few extra dogs, and before I knew it, I was up to fifteen dogs. Martin never said a thing. And then, I'm not sure how, the number crept up to twenty—still he never said a thing—and before I was done, I had a kennel of *thirty* dogs camped out in the Buser kennel.

I really didn't intend to push all of Martin's buttons, but that's what I did. My excess dog population and my own personal view of the world were just too much. The last straw was my partying ways affecting his dogs' care. On Friday nights, I didn't have much difficulty finding a good party, and my conscience wasn't very well developed either. I was supposed to water the dogs at seven in the morning, but I might not get to it until noon, and to tell you the truth, it didn't bother me. After one too many times, late that fall, I left on a sour note.

Martin and I loaded my dogs into Martin's dog truck and he motored out behind my car as we traveled down the long dirt road

I looked at Tonya then back to the doctor, thinking, "What the hell?"

"What?" is all Tonya could say. She was turning white. It was six o'clock in the morning, just an hour after I finished my first Iditarod.

The doctor went on to explain that the problem was much more serious than an abscess, and he advised me to see an ear-nose-throat specialist. The Iditarod Finishers Banquet was the next day, a Sunday, and we stayed for that. But on Monday, Tonya and I were headed back to Anchorage. My parents and family knew something was wrong, but I wasn't giving out any information.

Before leaving Anchorage for the drive down to Kasilof, we stopped at Mom's house, where I was disagreeable, mean, argumentative, grouchy, and miserable to be around. I remember my mother saying, "Whoa, Lance . . . *who are you?*" I didn't tell her what we'd learned in Nome, but several days later Tonya called her with the details.

In Kasilof, we met again with Dr. Zirul, who continued to act as our advisor and advocate. It seemed like I'd been pushed in and out of doctors' doors in the previous year, but now Dr. Zirul was ready to act on our behalf. He immediately asked for other opinions from his colleagues in Soldotna, and it was Dr. Zirul who brought us into a little chapel in the Soldotna Hospital.

With tears in his eyes, he told us how sorry he was for his initial diagnosis. I knew what he was going to say, and I had to hold Tonya's hand. It was a complicated cancer of the throat and jaw that required immediate attention. In his opinion, it didn't appear that anyone in Alaska was prepared to perform the radical surgery required, and therefore he recommended that we relocate immediately to Virginia Mason Medical Center in Seattle.

Then some new information landed in the mix. We were told that a young doctor in Anchorage, just thirty-four years old, had called and was prepared to handle the surgery if we wanted to stay in Alaska. The baby-faced Dr. William Fell, we would learn later, was the same age as me.

With this development, I asked, "Can my wife and I talk about this a while?" Tonya and I went over the pros and cons of choosing either Anchorage with a young doctor, or the prestige and history of

Virginia Mason in Seattle. Besides the urgency of our decision, I had to consider the overwhelming additional cost of moving to Seattle.

I wanted to stay in Alaska and felt strongly about it. Tonya's feelings were mixed, but she agreed with my logic. Dr. Fell was a young guy trained in the latest techniques, full of energy, and besides, I liked his confidence. He said he could do it. Within an hour, I decided to put all the chips on the table for a life-and-death gamble with Dr. Fell.

Once I settled on a decision, Tonya backed me. With that, Dr. Zirul, my doctor in Soldotna, immediately asked if he could be a part of the Alaska team and help organize what could be a delicate project.

The flow of events in my life had once again accelerated, giving me a view of a future that was even more compressed. I was just an average person, I thought, placed in an unusual predicament. It seemed time had no meaning, unless you grabbed it in the moment. I still had this wonderful vision that I could create something unique and beautiful for the world.

With the announcement of my illness, emotion gripped my mother, who'd always seemed so in control, and my father, so strong and driven. All of the family contemplated the possibility I may not make it.

Surgery was scheduled for April 6. But that didn't stop Tonya from putting on a pair of rubber boots and a raincoat, and wading out into the spring rain, the slop and the mud of the yard, to feed the dogs. In spite of the crisis, she knew my vision was real. Tonya never said a word while she held the family together. She just made sure that six females were bred to Zorro, my big, indestructible, strong, enthusiastic yearling that had pulled me to Nome. I would have my yard of pups when the snow started to fall.

ON APRIL 6, 2001, barely three weeks after my rookie finish in Nome, when the Alaskan sun was hanging in the sky more than twelve hours a day and starting to melt the snow in Anchorage, I entered the hospital for surgery.

It was an emotional time, and not just for me. I later learned that Mom and Dad were advised that I may not come out of the operating room, and it would be prudent to set everything right before I was sedated.

The irony was that my rock-solid father was a mess, emotionally unsupportable. My mother struggled to maintain strength and composure, and Tonya was fighting to stay optimistic. She knew there would be a lot of sorrow and tension in the family, but she'd said, "If this is his last memory, we have to give him something happy."

I was aware in a distant way that friends and family were preparing for the worst eventuality. As I was rolled toward the operating room, stretched out on the gurney, Tonya pepped me up with, "Honey, give 'em hell, I'll see you when you get out. You'll be all right." She even told me I'd run the Iditarod again.

My mother, trying her best to appear calm, said, "You can put the ball away, or you can give it your best shot." She was never ready to quit, and neither was I.

At the last moment, I told her, "Mom, you just have to keep it together."

"I know it, and I will," she said. A minute later, as I disappeared down the hall, the waiting room full of family and friends lost all composure and broke down and bawled.

Meanwhile, in a different frame of mind, Dr. Fell was seriously preparing to get to work with his team. I always think of Fell when I'm in the middle of some hard work, and I realize that sometimes you have to be the person who just knuckles down and gets the job done. His team was getting ready to haul some very heavy freight.

My goal was to defy anybody who said 'can't.'

The surgery to remove the cancer was extensive, including the radical removal of the tumor and tissue in my right jaw and neck, and all my salivary glands. To remove the squamous-cell carcinoma, Dr. Fell removed most of a main muscle in my neck that supported my right arm, plus more tissue, including the interior carotid artery. Because the salivary glands protect the teeth, my rear teeth were removed. Theoretically, removing my rear teeth actually would extend the useable life of my front teeth.

In the days following surgery, I also had two very high doses of radiation. The radiation treatments were radical, an option that could only be used once. Since my cancer was in my throat area, the radiation was focused on my neck. Of course, many nerves radiate from the neck, so I had damage elsewhere, particularly in my hands, for example, that would be a lifelong consideration. Some consequences complicated the recovery, such as operating with dysfunctional taste buds and depending on thyroid medication for the rest of my life. That part also needs continuous monitoring through regular blood tests.

Over the next couple of years, many friends would confide and tell me they honestly didn't expect me to live. I think my family was thinking the same way.

I did emerge from surgery, however, a little altered, but still Lance Mackey. As my mother put it, "So the kid who made my life miserable made me ecstatic when he decided to live as an adult."

Given the advanced stage of my cancer, the strategy was to be really aggressive with surgery and radiation. Chemotherapy was not used, figuring chemo would be saved as a back-up option in the next scenario should cancer return.

When I woke up, I realized my head was wrapped as a big as a pumpkin—I looked like a monster character who'd just had a brain transplant. My jaw was wired shut so that I wouldn't disturb Dr. Fell's surgical reconstruction. I couldn't eat anything, except marginally through a straw, so a tube was installed just below my sternum for direct feeding into my stomach. The stomach tube was a huge inconvenience that I would rely on, almost exclusively, for more than a year. It basically just sucked.

As I regained a groggy appreciation of reality after surgery, Tonya was supervising my return to the living with her usual attention to detail. I didn't know it, but my face was black and blue, about two times its normal size, and it was hard for anybody to look at me without grimacing.

The doctor had told Tonya, "Nobody give him a mirror until the anesthetic wears off completely." Naturally, he wanted me to wake up to life with a neutral or even positive attitude. He'd added another directive quite emphatically: "I want him to have at least a couple of days so that the swelling starts to go down."

Tonya relayed this information to the family and was the buffer between me and the outside world. But it didn't take long for the game plan to unravel.

As soon as I could have visitors, my brother Rick came in. The first thing out of his mouth was, "Oh my god, Lance, you look like hell."

I was just starting to focus on reality, and I managed to mumble through my locked jaws, gangster-style, "Really? Get me a mirror."

Just to prove that I really was uglier than hell, Rick found a mirror and held it up so I could get a good look at myself. I admit, I was taken aback when I saw how I'd been modified.

Tonya, of course, blasted Rick, "You dumb shit, why'd you let him see himself?" Rick, from his point of view, thought he was just carrying out his brother's request.

"He *wanted* to see himself in a mirror," was his weak defense. Even at the time, I appreciated the humor. We all laugh about it now.

For the first eight days after surgery, I could barely walk, couldn't eat, and definitely needed twenty-four-hour care. The radiation treatments were intense. I hibernated in my bed, motionless, drawing on the reserves of my body. I lost a lot of weight. And it became clear that my body was not healing.

The surgery site on my neck was held together with staples. Doctors warned me that I would have to guard that side carefully for the rest of my life.

As a result, I was scheduled for a hundred and twenty hyperbaric oxygen treatments. Essentially, the treatments help the body if it's having trouble healing on its own. Oxygen is fed into a chamber at two to three times the normal air pressure so it can reach damaged tissues more efficiently. The schedule was three hours per day in the hyperbaric tube, five days a week, over the course of the summer. It did heal me, and I'm grateful. I know it was necessary. Yet I was fighting every minute to escape the limitations of my cancer treatments.

After the operation, I faced a continual dose of practical advice: you can't lift your right arm, you'll never run the Iditarod again, always keep your neck covered to protect the delicate tissue, you'll always have to have a water bottle to swallow, food won't taste the same, activities are limited, and a long list of other precautions and restrictions. Of course, one of my reasons for living has always been, "Don't tell me I can't," and from that time in the hospital, my goal was to defy anybody who said "can't."

At the same time I was seeing a steady stream of visitors, including lawyers who'd read about my medical journey and earlier misdiagnosis. They wanted to sue on my behalf in a malpractice medical suit.

As I got stronger, my attitude about suing hardened. I told them, "I am not about suing anyone. This was the doctor who got behind my problem and worked to find a solution. He was the one who helped put the team together to do my surgery in Alaska."

People ask me how I coped with those days. What was my attitude? Was I calm? Did I decide to trust the people around me while I recovered? The answer, for whatever reason, is NO. I was irritated, pissed off, and probably not a model patient in many respects. Days after surgery, I was irritated about being separated from my family, home, and dogs. I was particularly peeved and not happy about the requirement that I stay in Anchorage for daily treatments at the hospital.

I think it was part of the recovery. I was mad and I wasn't going to let the cancer beat me up—at least not more than I already was. It may have been another "me-against-the world" battle in which I was bent on proving them wrong about my future prognosis.

On a practical basis, my wife realized that the medical experts were correct, in the early stages of recovery, when I couldn't function independently. She also realized what I needed for myself: to start doing the things I'd been dreaming about before I underwent these procedures.

If my behavior may have seemed counterproductive to someone watching from the sidelines, Tonya understood that I was in the middle and needed to pump up my self-worth. The first business item I needed to address was seeing the dogs and making plans to race them.

I stubbornly wanted to follow our game plan, which was to run five Iditarods in a row and see where we could go with it. That was our goal. I wanted to give the plan a fair trial. If we weren't achieving reasonable success at the end of five years, then we needed to change directions and look for something else to do. The Iditarod is too expensive and time-consuming to settle for a mediocre result. I'll be the first to admit, though, that considering my health status, the odds were not good for a 2002 project and Iditarod number two.

In the meantime, my wife was working hard to keep a balance between what was necessary to keep me under medical supervision at the hospital, but also recognizing that I was getting depressed and wanted to bust out of there and go home.

Tonya went to the hospital director one day and discussed what she was seeing. I was given free access to morphine to control pain, and sometimes I was high on it, just staring out the window. I was high and I was low. I was also depressed, and there was little she could say or do that didn't bring a difficult response from me.

My usual outlook was, "This is bullshit. I just want to go home." I thought I could accomplish everything medically at home as easily as the hospital. I put her in an impossible position.

Tonya ran a great balancing game. She was trying to keep me in the hospital for as long as possible, but I kept pushing, "Let's just load me up, drive me out of here, and let's go home. I don't have to report to anyone." She had the common sense to keep me on track and under supervision while I healed, knowing I had to be at the hospital a minimum of three hours a day just for the hyperbaric treatments.

My wife worked out a deal with the director. She knew I needed a dog to keep me focused and bring me out of my low. *A sled dog in the hospital? That's prohibited*, she was told initially. But she persisted, explaining that it was part of my vision for the future.

"Just let me bring in one of his dogs for an hour, and see if that doesn't raise his spirits." After several rounds, she finally prevailed.

The only dog at home that could adapt to a hospital room setting was my black leader, Angel. Tonya called Kasilof and asked somebody to collect Angel and drive her up to Anchorage.

Angel arrived on June 2, a tremendous surprise for my thirty-first birthday. Seeing that dog was a big boost and created a lot of excitement. A photo of Angel's visit with me was later used in a Discovery Channel piece on my life story. There I was, blackened from radiation, a feeding tube emerging from my upper abdomen. Angel calmly sat next to me on the couch, clueless as to the importance of her visit. But for me, she was just the medicine I needed. According to my wife, life suddenly

Without my knowledge, Tonya pestered the administration until the hospital finally allowed a visit from my well-behaved Angel. She came to see me on my birthday.

became easier for her. That's all it took—a little fix and a reintroduction to my reality, and I was much easier to handle.

Now done with surgery and radiation treatments, the rest of my summer was spent trying to heal up and gain strength. The hyperbaric treatments, all hundred and twenty of them, were scheduled five days a week, so I would try to get out early Friday morning and in as late as possible on Monday. I couldn't wait to leave the hospital and drive my truck down the Kenai Peninsula to Kasilof. The worst part was over, and I could think about the family and the sled dogs.

By mid-August and September, I was starting to gain some strength, but not enough to handle some of my ideas. Often I'd sit in the truck with the heater blasting and just consider the dogs, while Tonya and the kids did the chores. Other times, I could be in one of those trances, staring at the dogs, not really aware of what I was thinking. My father believes this is when I looked deep into the nature of sled dogs and made some discoveries. He also thinks it saved my life.

I wanted to cart train on dry land in the cool fall weather before actual snowfall. However, I was just too whupped to even handle a dog to harness. Instead, I would organize my kids, who would hook up the dogs and line them out on a towline connected to my four-wheeler ATV. I'd just sit there—my only physical effort was to drive the ATV. An extra kid would come along to handle the occasional incident. Life was getting better with each 5-mile training run. My schedule was also becoming easier because

Amanda and Brittney, as small as they were, helped tremendously during my recovery, hooking up the dogs so I could go for short runs.

I would drive to Anchorage and stay at my mother's place between visits to the hospital for hyperbaric treatments.

I was in violation of doctor's orders on weekends. My family said I was in *gross* violation. I still had staples in my neck from surgery; the closed tissue was vulnerable and not healed. My doctors constantly reminded me of the danger, especially if my neck was to be traumatized again—even a dog jumping up on me could be enough to unravel my neck. "Please don't do it," was their advice.

Well, this is how I looked at it: I am not going to sit in the hospital and croak. I would rather be out on the four-wheeler with my dogs and do it that way. At least I was having fun doing what I wanted. So there was no telling me otherwise, and I continued to think about getting the dogs some preseason conditioning. Denying the doctors' advice may have been another way that I was also confronting the cancer. I honestly believe that the dogs helped me recover that fall and put me in the position I am today.

During the weekdays, Tonya took care of the dogs and the house, while the kids went to school. She was the backbone of the operation, working alone and physically completing tasks in the dog yard that were just time-consuming drudgery. Unless it was your project, keeping a dog yard is non-stop work, day after day, with a lot of heavy lifting and mucking around in mud, dirt, wet snow, and grime. Tonya was never rewarded with the excitement of racing or a wild training run with the dogs. She did it for me, and that is something you can't forget. That's love.

Healing for me was slow. Having lived through the experience, I really don't know what I could have done without the hyperbaric treatments to help me heal. My body just wasn't doing it on its own, and I never found any alternatives that would have helped in a similar way. The procedure was cold and lengthy. It felt like I was descending in a submarine to get pressurized, then there was the actual fifteen-minute treatment with straight oxygen, and then coming to the surface for decompression. That's why it takes three hours. I could watch television or listen to music to relax and pass time. I understood the importance of the procedure because I was still almost six months out of surgery and still held together with surgical staples. Also, I was still trying to gain weight and depending primarily on my stomach tube to consume most of my calories.

Dr. Fell became a part of my day-to-day life. I visited him often for check-ups and he became interested in my outcome far beyond just a doctor-patient relationship. In fact, he became a big contributor and sponsor to my Iditarod program for several years.

That's the thing. Every one of the doctors who worked on me and initially advised me against driving dogs or racing or participating in the Iditarod has gotten behind me and sponsored me. They realized it was part of my recovery, and I think they recognized and maybe admired my determination. Since they figured out that I was not going to go off course, they decided that they might as well be part of the recovery. I recognize now that they understood the risks if I fell off my sled or got brushed off on a bad section of trail. They knew I wasn't going to lay around waiting for appointments at the hospital and live half a life. Plus, if I made it, they wanted to be part of the success.

My radiation doctor put it this way: "You're taking your life in your own hands. You have very thin skin covering the side of your neck and a main artery that's dangerously exposed. It's taken over six months to heal. If you were standing in the emergency room with a team of physicians, and a dog jumped up and scratched your neck, we wouldn't be able to save you. So we probably wouldn't do a good job if it happened on the trail."

They offered to fit me with a plastic collar to protect the exposed area on my neck—sort of like the collar you see on car-accident patients.

"No, thanks," I said. I wasn't going to do it.

"Why not?"

"Well, I just don't want to pamper myself." I kept thinking I was going to follow my goal program, which meant we were running the kennel for competitive success, at the highest level, and I wasn't compromising. Simple as that, I convinced myself that going out at thirty-one with a smile on my face was better than holding back.

No doubt, I was a doctor's nightmare—a person they wanted to help, but one who refused to go along with all their precautions.

I do have a few things, other than just inherent risk, that I have to really think about while I am running. On the race trail, I am managing sixteen charged-up animals in exquisite physical condition, highly motivated to travel, and trained since puppies that there exists only one direction and that is up, over, and through obstacles in a forward direction. With an average weight of fifty-five pounds, this is a sixty-four-legged bio-machine weighing eight hundred and eighty pounds and traveling at an unstoppable 10 mph. They are quite capable, when a finch in the brush sings, or a snowshoe hare bolts, of instinctively surging to 20 mph or more. On a downhill, visualize "out of control and we're all going to die."

I've come up with some protective measures. If I flip over, for example, and I'm dragging behind the sled, I have to immediately let go with my right arm. It has to be an automatic reaction because I have limited mobility, especially over my head. I can move my right arm above my head slowly with help from my left arm, but it's a tight maneuver. If I jerk on my right arm in an overhead position, I'll definitely damage the surgically repaired side of my neck, probably tear it apart, and it could be life-threatening. It's so restricted in that overhead position that I have come to recognize immediately that I can't test the right arm.

Hanging on to the sled with my left hand or arm also creates some additional problems, aside from having to one-arm it. Radiation treatments have damaged nerves to my extremities, particularly leaving me with severe pain in my left index finger. Eventually, I just had the finger surgically removed, so that limits my grip to the remaining three fingers and thumb. I need them in good shape to help booty the dogs.

I also have this damn water bottle that has to be with me at all times. I can't function without it. So what if I can't turn my neck, or my arm is limited in mobility, or my hands and feet hurt a little? I can forget about it from time to time. But that damn water bottle is a constant reminder. I must have it to swallow, since I can't generate saliva, so it's not something I can ignore or overcome with mental toughness. I have to plan for a water supply at all times. That's just a reality.

One April, I was training some yearlings in warm temperatures. I had a little tangle and was working to straighten things out, when all of a sudden, in a space of thirty seconds, I realized that I wasn't going to be able to breathe unless I got a swallow of water immediately. I was gasping for air, and I didn't have my water bottle within reach. I had to abandon everything I was doing to scramble for that water—and that's a reality I cannot escape. In a racing situation it means I need bottles in the sled, extra bottles in an insulated cooler that won't freeze, and a bottle or two on my person in case I lose the sled. If I'm on the trail for a long time in cold temperatures, I can always cut the plastic off and start chipping ice cubes with my knife.

And I know what you're thinking. A sharp little girl in the sixth grade once asked me, "Lance, why can't you eat snow?"

Aside from the huge drain of calories to melt snow at -30°F or -40°F—a really bad habit—swallowing snow is extremely risky because I have no salivary glands and my mouth is dry. At cold temperatures the snow is like fluffy dust, and I could easily inhale the snow particles into my lungs. Believe it or not, I could drown.

On the big picture, outside my life as a musher, I realize that I have it easy. So many of my fans are way worse off than I am, and I'm constantly inspired by their stories and their determination. I would rather be living life this way with a few risks than diminish my goals. I just can't gripe.

In their eyes, I was bare-boned thin and exhausted.

unning the 2002 Iditarod was still on my five-year plan, regardless of my slow summer recovery. It seemed like we were constantly driving up to Anchorage for appointments with the hyperbaric chamber and hospital. Through it all, preparing for the Iditarod was one fact I could hang on to mentally.

Almost six months after my surgery, the first winter snow on the Kenai started to whiten the dog trails in October. At the same time, they finally removed the staples holding my neck together. I stayed focused on healing and proving that I could get back on a sled. A friend suggested an appropriate name for my sled-dog operation— The Comeback Kennel—and I was ready to live up to the name.

That summer I'd discovered something in me that I hadn't recognized before: an ability to make long-term goals and visualize them. After cancer, I'd come to realize how fast life can end, and that nothing is for certain. I seriously started prioritizing my experiences in ways I'd never done before. I had to choose which experiences were most important and also think about how I was going to accomplish them. I do it all the time now when I'm training pups, thinking of the future two or three years out, but also with plans for the kennel, my competitive racing goals, and even my personal finances—since that affects my goals.

I'd always had this vague notion that I was going to correct things that I'd done in the past and make my parents and friends proud. I

When there's no snow on the ground, I train the dogs using an all-terrain vehicle. I can apply braking power that I don't have with a dogsled. WALT TREMER PHOTO

knew that I'd been a disappointment in many ways. But my good intentions remained undefined and foggy—a general idea with no direction or definition.

After cancer, my mind clicked into another gear. I started asking myself what interested me, what goals would I set for myself, and what was I willing to sacrifice or suffer to attain them. I also started to acquire a skill that surprised even me. I would start with a goal, and then actually design a timeline to see how I was going to do it—complete with set points to that goal.

For the 2002 Iditarod, I was obviously facing some unplanned medical challenges to those set points on my calendar. Still, the Comeback Kennel was waiting for me with a group of veteran and mature dogs ready to race.

With my last hyperbaric treatments behind me, I started thinking about how I was going to get myself ready for the race. I had to transition the dogs from my four-wheeler trainer to the world of snow on a sled. I had a lot more dogs—enough for two training teams of twelve dogs. The Iditarod rules allow a maximum of sixteen in the team, and so my pool of twenty-four gave me a good cushion to select the ones that were ready to run.

Even though I was back and forth to Anchorage all summer, Tonya, with help from the kids, did a masterful job of raising Zorro's pups in addition to other litters from different parents. They also babied my yearlings from the previous summer—they'd be ready to race through the 2001–02 winter. It was unbelievable. The dogs were *my* passion. It wasn't my family's dream, but they just dug in and worked like they were building the pyramids in the backyard.

Mentally I was serious about running two teams a day and throwing in a 40-miler on a regular basis for endurance training. And whether or not I liked it, I was forced to develop strategies to deal with several medical realities. I had a blanket strategy that solved the dire warnings about overextending my right arm and shoulder, and exposing the fragile tissue of my neck to trauma. That is, I was simply willing to take the risk.

But lacking the ability to produce saliva, I constantly needed a water bottle for wetting my mouth and swallowing. It was the hundred-pound ball around my neck, something that could never leave my side. I was also still dependent for most of my calories on the feeding tube that was installed just below my sternum. Even though I was fuel-injected, so to speak, I was still having a tough time maintaining my weight six months after my surgery. I wanted to gain weight, but I just couldn't do it, leading friends and more than one sportswriter to tactfully describe me that year as "gaunt."

I had clear ideas for training. For conditioning, I wanted to take one team for a 40-mile run, eat lunch, and have the other team harnessed and ready to go for another training run. Unfortunately, I just wasn't set up to handle it physically. I was ground down before we started. As a result, training was taxing, tiring, and an uphill challenge.

My two wonderful girls, Amanda and Brittney, must have inherited their mother's intuitive understanding of my vision and freely offered their extra time. While Tonya worked, the girls and a neighbor, Tod Black, fed and took care of the dogs, cleaned the yard, and essentially ran the kennel.

The girls harnessed the dogs, and I was just dead weight for the ride. When I normally would have jumped off the four-wheeler or sled to correct a problem in the team, I had to tell the girls how to handle it or just ignored it. Little things, like making sure the dogs were working on their preferred side of the towline, or switching dogs around in the team to get a nice balance of working pairs, often went uncorrected. I had just enough energy to get around the training loop.

I kept thinking, "This is great mental training for Iditarod. I'll be tired on the Iditarod, so this is good for me." But it was just rationalizing—hopeful thinking.

About the time we could get on snow with a sled, I could still hear the doctor's cautionary advice in the back of my head, "Don't do it, don't do it . . . ," but I went ahead and did it anyway. The main limitation was energy. I had enough to run the first team, but not enough for the second. The first team usually ran the number of hours or miles I wanted, but the second team always got shorted. If I was supposed to get a 40, the second team might only get 20.

It seemed like I ran every day. But often the 50-miler I had in my head ended up a 10-miler. At times, I was training one team every other day despite all my big plans. I just didn't have the zip to manage the dogs. It was a constant mental effort to overcome my own physical fatigue.

In the interim, I had this little consideration called finances. Tonya was still working, but I'd been out of commission in a hospital when I was supposed to be fishing all summer. Beyond willing myself to work with the dogs, I wasn't in any shape to get on a payroll or someone else's schedule. And without my doctor's work release, I don't think anyone would have dared hire me. For a while, I collected Social Security Disability. That took us over the edge so we could actually pay our bills.

Fortunately, as I prepared to run the Iditarod, Dr. Fell, Dr. Zirul, and my radiologist, Dr. Richard Chung, stepped up to financially support my effort. Of all my creditors, I owed those docs the most, and yet here they were taking a personal interest in my recovery to support me. Other people came out of the woodwork to help. Ralph and Laurie Calkins, good friends, organized a benefit fund-raiser on the Kenai that was a big success. People I didn't even know donated money and time to help my Iditarod effort. My mother also helped in a major way and put up real money for the race.

All these gestures were overwhelming and unexpected. It was an extremely tight budget, but it did get me to the start line. Of course, I've never needed a whole lot of extra. I've always managed to get by with what I needed and nothing more—and that's the way I did it in '02. If I needed booties for twelve days, then I probably had ten-and-a-half days' of booties, and that was enough to make it. The Booty Brigade, a group of race fanatics who sewed booties, gave me a good supply, and John Cooper, a retired musher who actually manufactured booties in Thailand, cut me a good deal. If I bought a hundred dollars' worth of booties, he'd give me the thousand-dollar discount. Other friends made dog coats—necessary if the weather turns sour, especially on the Bering Sea Coast. And then we charged the airline tickets to Nome for Tonya and the kids using our Alaska Permanent Fund Dividend checks.

The Iditarod gives fans an opportunity to ride through the streets of Anchorage in the sled of their favorite musher at the Ceremonial Start. The Iditarider program is a popular fund-raiser, with potential "Iditariders" paying thousands for an online bid to join their musher on race day. My 2001 Iditarider, hearing about my battle to get to the start of the 2002 race, came forward and generously paid my entry fee, a significant sum at $3,500.

Fortunately, I was also offered some low-cost or no-cost dog food that was great for the dogs, especially in training. I had good local sources of fish—mostly salmon—and the occasional horse carcass, an excellent quality protein the dogs needed to perform at a high level. My biggest problem was a source of commercial kibble, which gives the ration a good nutritional base. I was feeding a grocery store special that I could buy for twenty bucks a bag. It was a decent 30 percent protein, 20 percent fat kibble, and in combination with the fish and meat, we managed to keep the dogs in good shape. In fact, they were fat, simply because I just wasn't putting the miles on them like I wanted. On the race trail, however, I knew I would need a high-quality, but expensive, commercial kibble. I bought just enough of the high-quality race ration for my checkpoint bags that were sent out on the trail. And not a kibble extra.

We didn't have extra anything, that's for sure, and everything we accumulated went to the 2002 Iditarod. The dogs had lots of energy, and I was just plain tired.

I was determined to run the race even though I still had the stomach tube in place. I was incapable of eating little more than mushroom soup on my own. Even at the start of the Iditarod in March, almost a year after my cancer treatment and surgery, I was still on the trail fuel-injected. (If I'd have won, somebody would have said I had an unfair advantage, but I have trail-tested a stomach tube, and believe me, it's not the new secret to outwit your competitors.)

With persistence and help, I managed to prepare gear and food drops for the race and get us all to the start line on March 2, 2002. You could fairly say I was a physical wreck, but mentally, I was okay. Having finished the Iditarod in my rookie year, I'd learned the trail. This year, I had a little better dog team with some two-year-old dogs that I'd raised myself, plus a few new mature dogs I had borrowed. I considered my 36th-place showing in 2001 a laid-back camping trip. What could I do with a more competitive effort and planning?

THE 2002 IDITAROD was my year to actually race, and I took it seriously from the start, hanging with the front pack and arriving in Rohn checkpoint in 23rd place on the third day. Robert Sørlie, the Norwegian champion, was in 21st; Mitch Seavey, a Top 10 racer, was in 17th; and my good friend from Kasilof, Timmy Osmar, was in front of me in 22nd. I was in good company to break into the Top 20 and still had time to pump food down my stomach tube. I was on a competitive schedule.

Also I had made it through what many regard as the physically toughest part of the race. The trail crosses the Alaska Range, which

Tim Osmar and I napping in our sleds at Rainy Pass on Day 2.
JIM LAVRAKAS / ANCHORAGE DAILY NEWS

runs east and west and divides Alaska in half. We'd crossed the Range
at Rainy Pass, just west of North America's tallest mountain, Mount
McKinley. I got over the Alaska Range with a charged up dog team,
through some really challenging trail that descends to the Happy
River Valley and a deep defile that leads off the north side of the
Range through the Dalzell Gorge.

At the checkpoints, I was stopping to thaw out cans of Ensure,
my liquid food, just as I did at home. I'd put it down my feeding
tube for my main meal, and get back on the dogsled at below-zero
temperatures. My entire personal meal operation, however, was
gradually unraveling because my Ensure was frozen, and I needed a
warm place to pump it into my stomach. That was almost more work
than taking care of the dogs.

The feeding tube emerged flat on the upper part of my stomach.
But before I could eat, or inject, or whatever you want to call it, the
food into my stomach, I had to carefully warm those frozen cans.
The procedure called for attention to detail because the Ensure was
transferred to a syringe and then slowly eased into the stomach tube.
The liquid flowing into my stomach produced a weird and unnatural

feeling—I could actually sense the process. Oddly enough, one of the hazards of this procedure is drowning if you don't watch it and feed yourself too fast. Feeding requires patience and a slow, deliberate rhythm. At the least, you'll give yourself cramps, gut aches, and cold sweats if you try to hurry. Your stomach is designed for a slow input.

It was tough to find a place to do that in a checkpoint. Skwentna is a big one-room log house. Finger Lake is a tent set up on the margin of the lake. Rohn River is a twelve-by-fourteen-foot log cabin big enough for a single trapper, yet keeping fifty Iditarod people warm and supplied with coffee. Nikolai is a school gymnasium. McGrath is the city hall at its busiest day of the year when the Iditarod arrives. Spectators, officials, the media, pilots, and mushers mill in and out of checkpoints at all hours.

The real challenge, however, was on those long wilderness stretches between checkpoints. As best I could, I'd park the dogs on the side of the trail and find a place out of the wind on the trail, warm some Ensure using my alcohol dog-food cooker, and refuel like a race-car driver at a pit stop.

Physically it was tough, but mentally I figured I could do it if I just kept my head in the game. I found out it just wasn't good enough to think it. I just couldn't keep up with the calorie demands of the trail and the weather and, admittedly, I probably looked very thin. My body was begging for calories.

At Rohn, about 272 miles up the trail, I faced another eye-opening realization. I was the weak link—and because of that, my dogs did not have adequate pre-race conditioning. If I was going to run this race the right way, I needed to examine and think about how I was going to train the team. Good intentions weren't enough. Thinking about the effort wasn't enough.

I left Rohn with twelve dogs to carry me 90 tough miles through the Buffalo Tunnels, an arctic jungle of willow thickets wallowed out by a local herd of buffalo, and across the Nikolai Burn, a wide expanse of fallen timber and stumps left by a massive fire in the 1970s. I declared my mandatory twenty-four-hour rest in the Athabascan Indian village of Nikolai.

Iditarod rules require that a musher give the dogs a twenty-four-hour break somewhere along the trail. The choice of checkpoint is up to the musher. Normally, the front-runners go far beyond Nikolai, which is only at mile 347. It's not even a third of the way, so it's logical that the competitive mushers would want to go to a checkpoint closer to halfway before taking their big mandatory break.

Aside from allowing the dogs and mushers to have a nice rest, it gives the Iditarod veterinarians the time to thoroughly examine each team. I decided to pull up short at Nikolai to give myself time to take on my calories. Hopefully, it would also energize my dogs, which were now paying the price on the trail for their lack of hard training miles.

Twenty-four hours later, I left for the old mining town of McGrath with a reduced dog team. I was now down to ten dogs. Inwardly I was embarrassed by my lack of preparation, especially at McGrath, where the crowd of spectators milled through the dog yard talking with mushers and looking over teams.

McGrath, about a third of the way to Nome, is a major Interior village and the main air hub for this section of trail, complete with refueling and even several inns for an overnight stay. For that reason, the McGrath checkpoint is a gathering place for reporters from the Associated Press, *Sports Illustrated*, the *Anchorage Daily News*, the *Fairbanks Daily News-Miner*, fans from all over the world, and the interested locals. It was a crowd I simply didn't want to face. Yet I felt the necessity to stay for another long rest, despite a relatively fast travel time from Nikolai. This took me completely out of the competitive running. Those guys to the front weren't even stopping in McGrath.

I kept my thoughts to myself, because I was so disappointed. I didn't want to talk to anyone, didn't really want to acknowledge anyone, not even with a nod. I just wanted to get the hell out of McGrath. It was agony. After an eleven-hour rest to get myself reorganized and fed, I left with nine dogs for the 22-mile run to Takotna.

It was an acceptable run, and I was moving—finally away from the media and fans. Then another dog came up gimpy, and I knew that dog was staying in Takotna and flying back to Anchorage to join the other dropped dogs. I signed in and out of Takotna in ten minutes and continued on 30 miles to the Ophir checkpoint with only eight dogs.

The remote Ophir checkpoint is simply an old cabin opened every year by the Forsgrens, a family with several generations in the mining tradition. Situated near the Innoko River, the cabin checkpoint is quiet and staffed with only a handful of volunteers and officials. A few mushers stop for a break at the cabin, where the atmosphere is relaxed and friendly. The old mining town of Ophir is deserted in winter, except for the annual passing of the Iditarod, and only sees occasional activity in the summer mining season.

This is where I finally faced the reality of the 2002 race. Nobody told me to quit, but officials encouraged me to think about calling it a year. I now realize that they were very concerned about my health. In their eyes, I was bare-boned thin and exhausted. At the same time, they didn't want to get in the way of my will to finish the race. For

An overhead view of an Iditarod musher passing through the old mining town of Ophir. A mile farther at Forsgren's, I finally made my decision.
JEFF SCHULTZ / ALASKASTOCK

of snacks, extra alcohol bottles for my cook stove, and a half bale of straw for bedding. While I was dragging my supplies back to the sled, Larry decided it would be a good idea to sucker-punch Hobo. Although the fight only lasted seconds, Hobo was out of the race. That fast.

I dropped Hobo, hobbling with a swollen front-left wrist, in the checkpoint with a vet, tied the half-bale of straw to the sled, loaded the feed bags, and was in and out of Rohn in twelve minutes. I was leading the race, but I was really pissed at Larry for fighting, disgusted with Hobo for getting involved, and in the middle of a personal letdown. The team was plain, pathetic, lackluster. Larry was my brains, but Hobo was my speed leader, and I was really counting on him to energize the team. It got to me for a while, but then I realized it was affecting the team. I decided to get over it and improvise without him.

The warm weather and soft trails continued to slow every team, but I was really frustrated with mine. Every checkpoint was like a major event working with the race veterinarians. It seemed like every dog at one time or the other had a different variation of the creeping crud. Very quickly, I was getting a crash course in trail medicine. Fortunately, my instructors were the best canine athlete doctors in the world.

I had never been confronted with such a dismal situation. Of course, I had a dog or two get sick on the trail in previous races, but to have an entire team at various stages of recovery was very frustrating. Several times I almost felt like bagging it and even talked about scratching in Galena. To watch my team, subdued, picking at food, and moving down the trail with limp tug lines was disheartening, especially when I knew their capabilities. Where were my fireballs of energy that could blow through any obstacle?

I'm not big on using drugs unless I absolutely have to use them. In addition, the Iditarod has strict rules and testing on drug use, especially ones that might enhance performance. But I did learn how to use metranidazole, for example, and different antibiotics like antirobe, cephlex, and keflex at varying dosages to control stomach problems.

Of course, I knew there were different bacteria and viruses operating, but not how to pinpoint and control them with specific treatments.

I had to really baby the team, yet we were leapfrogging to the front of the race in a pack of eight or ten competitive teams. At Mc-Grath, I was 1st in and out with fifteen dogs instead of sixteen, thanks to Larry knocking out Hobo. Already, a theme was beginning to develop. My main contender, the four-time champion Jeff King, was 2nd with sixteen dogs, and by all accounts, a faster team. It seemed, even that early in the race, he was locking onto my tail, letting my team lay down the scent trail at the front of the race. He could keep on my rear with little stress to his leaders. He was shadowing me, the old strategy of the hunter on the trail of the prey.

It was an unusual predicament, and there was really nothing I could do to get out of it. My team was operating on half throttle, while normally my strength was the ability to make giant runs with a minimum of major rests. If I slowed down, King might take the opportunity to surge ahead and I might never catch him. Therefore, I decided to baby the dogs to the front, hoping that they would eventually work out of their funk. Fortunately, I had conditioned the team to travel on a fresh trail.

In hindsight, for the sake of the reader's understanding of this race, my mother has her own views. She thinks King made a big mistake by not letting down the hammer right there and then and taking control of the race. I was pretty vocal about expressing my frustration with my team. Some fans, suspecting a trap, have argued that King never trusted me and thought my team was more powerful than I was advertising.

At any rate, the race developed into a true cat-and-mouse contest between Jeff and me. Other players were in the mix, including Kjetil Bachen from Norway, Mitch Seavey, and my friend from Kasilof, Paul Gebhardt, but nowhere was the strategy so obvious. King was on my butt, always within an hour of reaching out and taking the lead.

By Ruby, the first village on the Yukon River, we had accumulated a two-and-a-half-hour lead. However, the lead time fluctuated, and it appeared that King was playing me with a faster team, always resting for fifteen or thirty minutes longer, and then regaining time on the next run between checkpoints. He reeled me in, yet never took the lead.

I remained frustrated with the team and missed the familiar surging and unstoppable power. Over the last several days, however, I felt the dogs were recovering, starting to eat with more enthusiasm, and leaning into the harness. The speed wasn't there for my outfit, but we were still a contender when King finally took an hour-and-a-half lead at Unalakleet on the Bering Sea Coast.

Finally, King had taken the initiative and was leading the race on the final 219 miles to Nome. He had sixteen dogs, an incredible accomplishment of dog care this far into the race, while my team was now reduced to twelve. He outnumbered me in team dogs, and appeared to be the fastest. Still, there was a glimmer of hope. My dogs were gradually gaining their familiar strength.

King returned to his hunter-prey strategy and allowed me to leave Shaktoolik first. He was still cautiously resting his dogs and waiting for the moment to take control of the race with his larger team. He left sixteen minutes later and, of course, intended to make up time on the next 48-mile crossing on the sea ice of Norton Bay.

I climbed off the sea ice and arrived at Koyuk at 1:19 P.M. on the eighth day of racing. King arrived minutes later at 1:27 P.M., having made up eight minutes on that crossing. In Koyuk, I still was vocal with the media, fans, and officials about my continuing frustration and disappointment with the team. Some race followers have theorized that I intentionally did this as a ruse. (Nobody ever asked me.) Whatever was the truth, King allowed me to leave Koyuk for Elim and then followed, as he had done throughout the race, exactly sixteen minutes later. Of course, he intended to follow the scent trail of my team and make up time, while at the same time letting his dogs rest a few more minutes in the checkpoint at Koyuk.

On the way to Elim, I was thinking of a million ways to get a little break: *If I could just get a fifteen- or thirty-minute advantage, I might have a chance to win the race.*

If you look at the map of the Bering Sea Coast, you can see that the distance from Koyuk to Elim to White Mountain is 86 miles. Many front-running mushers in past Iditarods have taken short breaks in the final miles of the race and gone from Koyuk to White Mountain in one run. It certainly was within the capabilities of my team, especially since they were feeling better, and I'm sure King was thinking I might try it.

Instead, I decided to take a gamble, after thinking about his strategy. I arrived in Elim at 00:47 A.M. and quickly unpacked my sled, left the sled bag cover open, and immediately started my dog cooker. I made every attempt to create the appearance that my team was done in, washed up, exhausted, and I was staying for an extended rest at Elim. Gear was thrown out of the sled-bag on the snow. White steam from my cooker formed a fog, especially with the light from a headlamp, and it looked like I was serious about staying. Even my attitude, I think, must have indicated that I was stuck on staying in Elim.

King arrived three minutes later, having made up thirteen minutes on the 48-mile run, and he still had sixteen dogs. Seeing that I was going to stop, he also parked his team and unpacked his sled. What had become an irritating behavior of tailing me the whole race had become predictable.

Both of us fed dogs, laid out straw for the dogs, and then went into the Elim community fire hall to warm up, eat some food, and finally, to take a little nap. I hung up my red suit on a hanger on the wall of the fire hall and settled in on the floor, my head against the wall. I was thinking about casually getting up, like I was checking on the dogs, leave my suit on the wall, and go out and leave with the dogs. If my suit was there, King might think I was still in Elim. Even a fifteen-minute breakaway might be enough to change the race. But my feet and hands were really hurting, especially since I had nipped my feet in cold weather on the Yukon Quest. Even though the weather was right at freezing and relatively warm, I figured it was just too dangerous to leave my outer suit.

For days I'd been daydreaming about a break, an incident that would give me just enough time to make a getaway to the front, and how it would unfold. What happened at Elim was so perfect, I could not possibly have scripted it. King settled in against the wall of the fire hall, close to me, his iPod plugged into his ears for some white noise, crossed his booted feet, and folded his arms on his chest. In about ninety seconds, he started breathing hard. I had been lying there, with my eyes closed, waiting for that sound.

I got up as carefully as possible, with my finger on my lips, looking at every one in the room to let this event play out on its own. I didn't want somebody screaming, "Lance, are you leaving?" For sure, the media and officials had been instructed over and over that they were not to interfere in the competition.

Quietly, I grabbed a cup of coffee, took my red suit off the hook, shut the door carefully, and eased outside to the dogs. All fall, all winter, since they were pups, I had been training for this moment with a training regime of unpredictable hook-ups. For this one moment, I was going to ask the dogs to believe in me and get off their beds for another 50-mile run. The tug lines were still attached to the harnesses, so I was instantly ready to depart. I tossed in a few gear items into the sled, closed the sled bag, grabbed the leader's neckline, and led them on the out trail.

I told the camera guy for Versus TV, "I am going to catch him, I'm gonna try and catch him with his pants down." I paused for a moment, then continued, "This is something you don't see very often." Then I told the cameras to cut the lights. The team trotted off into the darkness after a stay in Elim of exactly 1 hour and 33 minutes.

Over an hour later a snowmachiner came up to me with a report. Not knowing if I had five minutes or an hour on King, the stranger brought me up to date. King had left at 3:10 A.M. By the time he woke up from his nap and repacked his sled, I had fifty minutes on him. It was the oldest trick in the book, but it worked.

The "nap" incident at Elim has been recounted by a number of sportswriters and television reporters, and will probably be remembered in Iditarod history as a true classic. Apparently Jeff was pretty

Here's a view of imposing Topkok Hill, some 30 miles outside of Nome, when rookie Joe Gans and his team were covering the trail in daylight. Three days earlier, with King on my tail, I gave every ounce of energy I had to run uphill behind the sled and lighten the dogs' load. JEFF SCHULTZ / ALASKASTOCK

pissed off about finding himself as a main character in the history books, which is understandable.

I was driving eleven dogs, while King still had his outfit of sixteen dogs. Nevertheless, mine seemed to be gaining strength and, for the first time on the race, actually made time on King en route to White Mountain. After an eight-hour mandatory rest, eleven dogs and I departed with a time advantage of fifty-seven minutes. King was fifteen years older than me, but I decided that I was going to not leave anything on the table. By the time we crested Topkok Hill, running at every opportunity behind the sled, I had given all that I had. There was nothing left. I was sweating like a race horse and exhausted, and figured if King could overtake us in the next 30 miles to Nome, well, the race was his.

My eleven dogs, finally recovered and back with a spring in their step, crossed under the Burled Arch at 2:47 A.M. on March 12. Our total time on the trail was 9 days, 11 hours, 46 minutes, and 48 seconds.

An hour and nineteen minutes later, Jeff King, a guy I regard as the best musher in the world, arrived in 2nd.

The chaos and the celebration from the fans—and Tonya—at the finish was incredible. After the noise and excitement subsided, three things stand out in my mind about that race.

First, I proved to myself that if I am well enough to help the dogs, we could work our way through some serious difficulties, especially the health issues we faced early in the race.

Second, winning both the Yukon Quest and the Iditarod for the second time in a row, took the "fluke" out of the wind whispering in the trees.

Third, Jeff King is a class act, and I am honored to race with the man. He wanted to win as badly as I did, but he remained philosophical about the 2008 race and kept it all in perspective.

Mobbed by the media after my second back-to-back finish. JANET TREMER PHOTO

I met Jeff King under the Burled Arch when he arrived in Nome. A fierce competitor and gracious to the end. JEFF SCHULTZ / ALASKASTOCK

Zorro . . . didn't appear to be breathing.

I t wasn't over yet. Our hard work had paid off, our dreams had come true. Winning the two biggest races of dog mushing back-to-back, and twice, had made the history books, but there was still one more race waiting before the season was finished: the All-Alaska Sweepstakes, scheduled to start in Nome just two weeks after the 2008 Iditarod finish. The Sweepstakes was likely to be a once-in-a-career race for me, and I didn't want to miss it. The winner's purse, by the way, was advertised as $100,000—a real attention-getter.

The 2008 Sweepstakes was organized by the Nome Kennel Club and billed as a centennial celebration of the old All-Alaska Sweepstakes races held in Nome from 1908 to 1917. Nome was a baby boom town with plenty of interested gamblers. A tele-  graph line paralleled the trail, so the race was updated for the citizens betting the race on a chalkboard in Nome. The 408-mile race followed trails to the gold fields and camps on Seward Peninsula.

Competitors were well-financed by local enterprises, many of them in the gold business, and well-prepared for some spectacular races. Mushers included legends of the sport—"Iron Man" Johnson, Leonhard Seppala, and Scotty Allan, the "King of the Dog-Team Drivers," to name a few. Many of the dogs were Siberians purchased at great effort

Here's what Nome's Front Street looked like on April 1, 1908, with the first running of the All-Alaska Sweepstakes. Teams ran from Nome to Candle and back.
B.B. DOBBS COLLECTION, ASL-P12-103; ALASKA STATE LIBRARY

from Russia, and the early mushers had the financial backing to feed their dogs a king's banquet of lamb, butter, and other delicacies.

The modern-day trail followed the same 204 miles from Nome to Candle and back, with stops at seventeen checkpoints along the way. The Seward Peninsula is known for severe weather, especially wind that whips across the treeless tundra. Outside the checkpoints, mushers and teams are vulnerable in these elements. Some of the checkpoint names give you clues—Safety, Timber (hidden in a small cluster of stunted black spruce), Haven (out of the wind), and First Chance (your first and only chance to get out of the weather).

I had two short weeks between my Iditarod win and the Sweepstakes start on March 26 to reorganize and build a new team roster. My incredible team dog Zorro had been with me on our winning Quest just a month earlier. I owed a lot to the super-powered eight-year-old, and I wanted him on my Sweepstakes team. Plus, if you could ever have an animal for a friend, Zorro is mine.

Zorro was and is an incredible animal weighing in at a hefty seventy-five pounds. That's rare, since most competitive sled dogs weigh fifty to fifty-five pounds. But Zorro is a "franchise athlete" and can transform a team with his enthusiasm, work ethic, and unbelievable strength. Over the years, I've built my kennel genetics on him and my teams around him. In fact, nearly half the dogs in the Comeback Kennel are his descendents. He even has his own fan club, friends who wear a special patch that reads, "Who's Your Daddy?"

Zorro had helped me in my 2007 Iditarod win, too, even though I was pressed to drop him in the White Mountain checkpoint, where race veterinarians determined that Zorro had pneumonia. Personally, I didn't agree with the diagnosis, but of course I went with their professional decision and left him for a flight back to town. It was the first time ever that Zorro had been dropped for any reason in the seven years that we'd been racing together. He recovered quickly after that race, but it started me wondering if he might be in his last year of racing.

I'd had to drop Zorro at White Mountain in 2007 when he was diagnosed with a respiratory problem. My friend and fierce competitor, Paul Gebhardt, was standing by when I told Zorro I'd see him back at home. JON LITTLE PHOTO

Despite my reservations, Zorro was incredible in training and earned a place on the 2008 Yukon Quest team, where his seventy-five pounds of muscle was key to the race effort. Still I kept second-guessing him. I thought it wasn't fair to take him on the Iditarod, and then turn around and use him again two weeks later on the Sweepstakes. In

Leaving the start line for the All-Alaska Sweepstakes. The centennial race offered a first-place purse of $100,000. THERESA DAILY PHOTO

hindsight, I should have used him in all three races. He was that good, even at his age.

So Zorro sat out the 2008 Iditarod on Murphy Dome Road, along with several other Yukon Quest dogs, so he could run with me in the Sweepstakes. Preseason, my goals were realistic, and I was just looking for top finishes in the three big races. But if I'd had to choose just one to win, I'd have chosen the All-Alaska Sweepstakes.

Larry, my seven-year-old super-leader, came off the Iditarod limping, so he was out of the lineup. I left the rest of my Iditarod finishers in Nome to lounge around under Braxton's care. He drove them a couple of times for short distances, just to keep them tuned up.

Meanwhile, I flew to Fairbanks to train a group of Yukon Quest dogs and a few others I thought would do well in a 400-mile race. I then returned to Nome with essentially a new group of dogs to match up with the Iditarod dogs. Although a few of my key dogs were out of the picture, I thought I had a good core of nineteen dogs from which I could choose my team for the Sweepstakes race. Eventually I decided on thirteen solid dogs for the race, including Zorro, now nine years old.

My big oversight was underestimating the logistics of the race. I should have done my homework better. Usually, long-distance sled-dog races have rules that limit outside help to the musher. Assistance like a warm cabin or a big pot of moose stew is permitted if it's offered to all the mushers. But otherwise, a musher does all his or her own work. All basic chores like feeding dogs, putting on booties, or packing the sled are the musher's responsibility.

On the other hand, the Sweepstakes broke convention for self-reliance. In this race, you were allowed a snowmachine and crew to help set up camp, cook dog food, and help with chores. But it was my impression that the snowmachine could only travel ahead of the musher to set up camp. I found out later that the snowmachine and crew were actually allowed to travel along with the team, following behind if they wanted.

So I'd hired an airplane to haul my crew of two veterinarians and two handlers to two permanent camps that we'd set up with Arctic Oven tents. The result was that I had a camp about 65 miles from the start and 65 miles from the halfway point. I thought that was the best way to do it, and I didn't hire a snowmachine to join me on the trail, although others had.

To add to the confusion, there was a real lack of detail from the officials on what was and was not allowed. The rules were gray, and as a result, some mushers pushed it to the limit.

Jeff King, always a main competitor, hired two snowmachines and drivers to follow him and closely monitor his competition. I was surprised during the race when one of them pulled up alongside and the guy said, "We're working for the King, but we're rooting for you, Lance." Then he sped off, probably to give King an update on my speed and his time advantage.

At first I thought, "Whoa, are they trying to get inside my head?" but later, I figured the guy was probably a local from Nome and was telling me the truth. I found out I was right nearly a year later, when the man stepped up and introduced himself to me.

Lippy was one of my Golden Harness winners in 2007. I was studying her and other developing talent in the kennel as I looked toward the next big race.
THERESA DAILY PHOTO

knocking off Mackey, and I knew it. Mushers were closing the refrigerator door and not drinking that extra beer. Wives and husbands were advising their mate to get on the sled for another training run if they wanted to stick with Mackey. Computer screens were lit up late at night, mushers trying to fine-tune a schedule that would keep them to the front. Phones were ringing across North America as final deals were cut for key dogs to place in teams. And pundits, the newspaper guys who love to stir up controversy with outrageous predictions, were having a wonderful run.

In my mind, 2009 was set to be the sled-dog race of the century, full of the fury of Alaska.

CHAPTER 22 **2009 RACE MODE AND MY TEAM**

Anybody who said I was fading was wrong.

 onya, the dogs, the crew, and I drove 365 miles from Fairbanks to Anchorage for the 2009 Iditarod start. The shoulders of the Parks Highway were piled high with snow, backing up reports that the snow pack through the Alaska Range was deep. Joe Garnie's prediction looked right on.

For the first time in five years, I hadn't run the Yukon Quest in the middle of February. In the previous two years, when I'd won both the Quest and the Iditarod, I could feel the team's capacity for a thousand miles. I knew it. This year, I had lots of training and camping experience, but the team hadn't been tested by the Yukon Quest.

The longest run under any kind of test was a couple of weeks earlier when my stepson, Cain, took my nine best dogs to the Junior Iditarod. Cain had worked hard, he'd earned the right, and I wanted to see him do well on his fourth Junior race. Still, I was apprehensive. I made it clear that I wanted the team to look good when it came into the finish.

In the Iditarod, certain sleds are affixed with GPS trackers so fans can follow the mushers' positions online. There's no advantage for the mushers, because they're only transmitting; they're not allowed to receive any signals. This year, the trackers would be used for the first time in the Junior Iditarod. So Tonya and I rented a motor home, set up a computer, and camped at the finish line in Willow. I am not a tech guy, but I sat at that computer all night and watched Cain's little

Cain was ready, and I trusted him with nine of my best dogs on the Junior Iditarod.
DONNA DEWHURST PHOTO

GPS dot moving on the screen for 170 miles. It was nerve-wracking. I couldn't help comparing my best dogs to the other teams, and at times I wondered if he was moving too fast.

Just a year earlier, my father had been tracking my GPS dot on his computer screen in Arizona. He'd told an *Anchorage Daily News* reporter, "I'm drinking milk to settle my stomach. It's pretty nerve-wracking watching this thing by computer."

All my anxiety went away when I watched Cain and the team come in first with some of the dogs trotting and others slow loping. It was an exact photo of what I wanted to see. And hearing comments from the crowd at the finish was true satisfaction. Honestly, that win was the highlight of the entire 2009 racing season. I was so proud of his patience and skill. Then I remembered back in 1984, when my old friend Tim Osmar won the Junior. A few weeks later, his father Dean Osmar had gone on to win the Iditarod. I told Cain we were going to do the same thing. This year was ours.

I was really keyed up to race, and that's something you can't fake.

We expanded the house and the kennel—and our work in training novice mushers. Jamaican musher Newton Marshall stayed with us while we both trained for the 2010 Iditarod. THERESA DAILY PHOTO

Anybody who said I was fading was wrong. I was in race mode. From this point there would be little socializing. I was just as interested in beating new friends as well as old friends. Without being discourteous, I am totally focused on the dogs and what's going on around me.

The night before the start on March 8, I continued to cut back on the team's feed ration, because I wanted them sharp for the start. Hungry and a little edgy. I was also motivated to confront all kinds of dog-health problems based on my big learning experience last year. I'd had one dog with frostbite, but it wasn't a big deal, because I monitored him closely. Two dogs had had a split on a foot. It may sound bad, but it's no worse than a blister if you watch it. The tissue between the toes gets rubbed and tender from snow crystals. It's definitely uncomfortable, but detected and treated, that's an injury that can heal on the run, and it did.

A half-hour before our start time, I was still making decisions about dogs. My mother looked the team over and made some good observations. She asked what I planned to do about four females in heat, knowing they can be a huge distraction for the male team dogs. She advised me to not take them. But I'd been following events closely, and figured that two of the females would come out of heat in the first days of the race, and the other two would probably be done by the end of the race.

I'd also noted that two young males were wound up by those developments in the last few days, but they were still eating and pulling hard. It looked like the majority of the team was still focused on their jobs. I liked the team as it was, so I decided to take the females.

We were scheduled to depart in position number 47, which put us out at exactly 3:30 P.M. on that Sunday afternoon restart. On a strictly mathematical basis, it doesn't matter when you start. While the time difference between starting 1st and 47th is ninety minutes, it's all adjusted when we stop on the trail for a mandatory twenty-four-hour rest.

But in the real world, it does matter. The teams in front will chew up the trail in warm weather—so it gets slower when you're a follower. Plus my team should be passing some of the slower, less competitive teams. I was thinking about all these variables, but especially

Fans from all over the world flocked to the 2009 restart line in Willow.
AL GRILLO PHOTO

about keeping my leaders calm and conserving energy.

It was a crazy start in Willow. Spectators by the thousands lined against fencing out of the chute, while the dogs were lunging and acting ridiculous. My team pulled a crew of volunteers twenty yards down the trail in the start chute—just getting limbered up. I was jacked and they were, too. The trick was to keep calm.

Once we were on the trail that Sunday afternoon,

A frozen king salmon will be chopped into slivers for the two-hour snack breaks.

I was surprised that I wasn't seeing the teams that I figured we'd be passing. I was still watching Larry in the team just above the wheel dogs. He was trotting comfortably and kept telling me he was going to win the Iditarod. How could I doubt him? He's been the leader in ten 1,000-mile races and won seven of them. He's been awarded three Golden Harnesses. He's never been dropped with an injury or otherwise from any of those races. He's a superstar, a super-leader, even in the worst conditions.

On schedule, we were stopping every two hours for a snack break on the riverbed trail to Skwentna. Despite the initial excitement of the first day—which sometimes takes a team's mind off eating—mine were hungry.

We arrived at the Skwentna checkpoint at 10:27 P.M. in 19th place, which kept us anonymous in a big crowd of fast-moving teams. Obviously, I'd passed twenty-eight teams, but a lot of them were mushers who were simply camping alongside the trail. Trail mileage to Skwentna was 86 miles, and we'd done it in about seven and a half hours. At a little over 10 mph, Larry had set us on a classic marathon

Early in the race, I had to encourage a moose to give us the trail.
JEFF SCHULTZ / ALASKASTOCK

speed. Many teams were traveling much faster, probably over their heads, on that first evening.

After a perfect four-and-a-half-hour rest in the middle of the night, on the second day of the race, we departed Skwentna for the long, slow climb up the south shoulders of the Alaska Range. We climbed steadily for 75 miles.

About 20 miles short of Rainy Pass checkpoint, I suddenly realized there were no sled tracks ahead. I hadn't noticed that all the guys ahead had chosen to stop at Finbear Lake, just a little lake with a cabin. I really never intended to go to the front, especially with a start number of 47. Now I was the one leading the race.

I arrived first at Rainy Pass checkpoint around noon. We had traveled 75 miles on a slow, punchy trail in eight and a half hours. Not even a quarter of the way through the race at Rainy Pass, I had a good talk with DeeDee Jonrowe, the top woman Iditarod competitor. She's never won, but she's had fourteen Top 10s, one of those a 2nd-place finish. I told her it didn't matter who had the fastest team this time around—this year it was going to be tough dog time. She looked at me, thought about the trail we'd just seen, and agreed.

At this stage of the race, one thing going well for me was leader rotation. Because of the females in heat, I wasn't using a couple of distracted males to the front. Instead, I had Rev and Dred in the lead coming into Rainy Pass, but I was also switching out Maple, Zena, Battel, and a couple of others every two hours.

My biggest concern this year was the youth of my leaders. I remained cautious, because I didn't want to sour any of my superstars on miserable trail. It was just too much to lean on a couple of leaders, so I changed them out every two hours at the snack break.

I was very conservative and decided to rest for six hours in Rainy Pass—longer than any of the other front-runners. Team after team after team barreled through, but I had already decided to let the faster teams lay down the scent trail and save my surge for later.

This was my eighth Iditarod, and I could easily visualize the trail up and over the Alaskan Range and down the Dalzell to the north side. I was apprehensive about the Dalzell because I still had the power of all sixteen dogs, and I'd heard rumors of collapsed ice on the creek crossings.

Luckily, the Dalzell canyon wasn't as bad as described. Eight mushers ahead of me were laying down a nice trail on soft snow. In hindsight, the most impressive memory was my travel time with the Norwegian musher, Bjornar Andersen, and Cim Smyth from Big Lake, Alaska. From time to time I could catch a glimpse of them. Their speed was impressive—faster than I expected. I wasn't trying to race them, but truthfully, if I'd been trying to outrun them, I'd have had a hard time doing it. This was only the evening of the second day. I thought about it a while, and figured those dogs were the type that started out at 16 mph and finished at 6 or 7 mph.

I also had a chance to look over Jeff King's dog team, which was also in the front group moving down the Dalzell. I watched him on some of the downhills and noticed a difference in style between us. I noticed that King hardly used his brake and allowed his dogs to al-

Maple was juiced up to run. The little two-year-old female would really show her strength in the 2009 race. THERESA DAILY PHOTO

most free-fall on the down-hills—much more than I would have allowed mine.

At the next checkpoint in Rohn, Cim told me, "Man, King *travels* down the backside of those hills." It was possible King was making sure neither of us caught him at this stage. Or maybe it was just a psychological statement: "I'm driving the fastest team on the trail." It's one of those observations you roll around in your mind. Later in the race, what long-term sacrifices are you willing to make when you take the dogs out of their comfort zone, even for a while?

After all that deep snow and miles of maneuvering over Rainy Pass and down the Dalzell, we all came into the Rohn checkpoint practically holding hands. I was two minutes faster than King, but I never really intended for it to work out that way. All I could think about was surviving the next 20 miles out of Rohn, a very rough section of trail.

Rohn checkpoint is only a small cabin located in a beautiful stand of tall white spruce tucked in at the confluence of the Titina River and the South Fork of the Kuskokwim. Conditions are great in the protection of the checkpoint, but a hundred yards away, the trail emerges on to the smooth ice, sand drifts, gravel, driftwood frozen into ice and gravel, like giant traps for a sled-breaking accident. There is an ever-present wind funneling down the river.

Fortunately, a couple of guys had laid down a scent trail ahead of me—my old friend Paul Gebhardt, who's not afraid to push the race, and Sebastian Schnuelle. That was perfect. My new rule was to be conservative this early in the race and leave the checkpoint after another team lays down the trail.

Not only that, but my two best command leaders were males, and neither wanted to stay out in front because of the two females in heat, a development that my mother already predicted. My females were natural athletes and good front-end dogs, but they didn't have extensive experience. Still, I had to count on the females, and luckily they just shined, particularly a little two-year-old female named Maple.

Not only did Maple want to lead, she wanted to take control herself at the front. This is unusual for one of my dogs. Out of respect, I always try to ease the pressure of leading by pairing two dogs. But she told me herself, "No, Lance, this is going to be different. I want to run this team by myself." She gave me a whole new train of thought.

Trail conditions continued to be punchy, wet, soft, and slow going with temperatures to 40°F, that's above zero, for the next several hundred miles to Takotna. The dogs, all sixteen of them, were ridiculous at every snack stop, hammering their harness, whining, and barking all the way.

We'd heard there was two and a half feet of snow on top of the trail between Takotna and Iditarod. The trailbreakers were set to go ahead, but the big question was the warm weather. How long would it take for the trail to harden? Along with the rest of the pack, I immediately declared my mandatory twenty-four-hour rest at Takotna. It was the only sensible decision—nobody wanted to break trail for 100 miles. If you gambled and left ahead of the pack on bum trail, you just blew the race. The rest of the mushers might not say it out loud, but they'd be thinking it: "What a dumb move."

I started considering our position during the twenty-four break. We were almost a third of the way through the race. The front pack included Sebastian Schnuelle, Aaron Burmeister, Hugh Neff, Martin Buser, and Jeff King, the guy I considered the main threat. But I felt my team was getting stronger with each mile and might take control of the race if I could find a place to uncork them for a big run.

The warm weather was good for me personally, giving my hands and feet a break from the cold. I carry such a low body-fat percentage that I really have to pay attention to warmth and hydration. I probably had three hundred and fifty hand-warmers in my gear bags along the trail, and I was still using them three or four at a time in each mitt, even when it was warm. I was keeping up with my water intake, but even if you're fifty pounds overweight, the dangers of dehydration are real. If you're dehydrated, even slightly, you're more likely to become hypothermic. And if you're mildly hypothermic, you make bad, fuzzy decisions. It's just bad strategy to be either dehydrated or hypothermic.

Especially after cancer, I've had to work at keeping weight on. I've been able to get up to one hundred and eighty pounds, yet it's really easy to slide to one hundred and fifty pounds. So I took full advantage of the hospitality in Takotna. In twenty-four hours, I had six major meals. Between meals, I sampled the homemade pies, which are world-class, and kept the edge off until the next meal with some light snacks. My calorie intake seems ridiculous, but I burn it off so fast. I have to plan for it. I'm thinking about eating months before the race and remembering every checkpoint that has hot food. Many of the villages roll out a great selection of Alaska Native foods with salmon, moose, caribou, and berries. I say yes to every invitation.

Usually the Iditarod field is all over the map for the twenty-four-hour mandatory, but this year we were all in Takotna, except for Martin Buser in Ophir. The atmosphere was polite and cordial with a lot of joking around, which is not unusual. It's also possible to have an uptight checkpoint. All of us have trained all year, and nobody wants to roll over and play dead, and not take the race seriously.

So every conversation in Takotna included some probing: "How's the trail to Iditarod?" "How far can you go breaking trail every day?" and "What do you think Buser is thinking in Ophir?"

My departure time from the Takotna twenty-four-hour break was 4:46 A.M., March 12, a little more than an hour behind Aaron

Burmeister, Hugh Neff, and Sebastian Schnuelle. I'd looked at the checker's sheet and seen that I was the only front-runner still running sixteen dogs. At this stage of the race, it was anybody's.

My intention was to make the easy 25-mile trip from Takotna to the abandoned mining town checkpoint of Ophir, quickly check in and out, then continue 90 more miles to Iditarod. So we were looking at 115 miles of trail before getting to a warm place to dry out. The accepted race plan is to travel to a stop just short of halfway and camp—usually at a well-known little plywood shack called Don's Cabin.

We passed Schnuelle on the way to Ophir. Because no one was giving me any good information on the trail, at Ophir I'd loaded a bale of straw, a hundred pounds of snacks and meals for the dogs, some personal gear, and fuel for my cooker. That was enough for two major stops, if the trail was slow.

Even hauling the extra weight, it seemed like the dogs were going faster. The trail was also improving by the minute and starting to harden. It quit snowing, the clouds covered the sun, and the temperature stayed cool enough for the dogs to work in midday. The team and I passed my old Yukon Quest friend Hugh Neff traveling on the trail, but it happened so fast that neither one of us had a chance to talk. I remember Hugh yelling, "Nice-looking team. Have a good run!"

As always, we never missed the two-hour break, which is like a little party for the team, and then continued on a trail threading a vast landscape of tundra and stunted black spruce. Before I knew it, we found my old Quest buddy Aaron Burmeister camped at Don's Cabin, with his dogs on straw and a fog of steam surrounding his cooker. He was the leader of the race and seemed to be following the traditional strategy of stopping for a four-hour break. Again I was so focused on passing without any stutters or slowing the team down, that we barely had a chance to say anything but, "Hey, see you later!"

I never want to be involved in a big camp cluster, so my habit is to go a mile or two beyond a camp. On this section of trail, I knew about a little grass lake beyond Don's that would be perfect—a quiet, solitary place. As always, I'd be injecting doubt and unpredictability into my strategy.

Those few miles beyond Don's gave me a preview of the trail, and I'll be darned if the trailbreaker's trail wasn't setting up perfectly. The dogs were staying on top of the new crust, and gliding, not wallowing through loose snow, and I was at the front of the race—the place everybody was afraid to occupy. That made the move a good intelligence report. The uncertainty of the pack was now my advantage.

I'm never afraid to listen to the dogs, and in that respect I am a risk-taker. I spend so much time with them in training that I can almost feel what they're thinking. They were just going ballistic, lunging in harness, barking and crying—they were telling me they were not interested in camping. I figured we had traveled about 60 miles since Takotna and had another 45 miles to Iditarod.

To me, time alone in the middle of the Alaskan wilderness with a big string of noisy dogs is heaven. The dogs voted to go.

We made it from Takotna to Iditarod, a distance of 115 miles, in twelve and a half hours, arriving just before dark with all sixteen dogs pulling. I don't think anybody has done it that fast, even on an advertised fast trail. It was a phenomenal experience, and I was ecstatic and just amazed at what the dogs accomplished, especially on the fifth day of racing. Some of the superstars were trotting with the veterans, then erupting into a run, trying to speed up the team like rolling thunder. Bruce Lee, commentator for the Versus Network television crew, was in a helicopter following us into Iditarod. He later told me it was awe-inspiring to watch that team roll into Iditarod. I really enjoyed uncorking the team for that run. It also put us in the lead, as close as I could figure, by about four hours.

After a big six-hour rest, we left Iditarod for the 65-mile run to Shageluk, a small village on the banks of the Innoko River. I was actually kidding myself, "Lance, it's going too good with sixteen dogs. Keep alert and watch out."

I was planning on a traditional run to Shageluk and stopping for a rest in the checkpoint. The trail is often hard pulling on sugary, wind-blown snow, and gradually climbs over a series of big domed hills.

Going into Shageluk in those early-morning hours, I was really tired. I kept nodding off. It was hard work to stay awake. Sleep is my known personal negative. I know it and think about it all winter as a strategy item, just like any other limitation. Using a traditional stand-up sled helps me stay awake, and I've never used a sit-down sled, like many mushers do. This dark morning, all I could think about was stopping and napping for a couple of hours.

I ran behind the sled every once in a while to shake off sleep, and at last we pulled into Shageluk just as it was getting light. When I stopped the dogs to sign in with the checker, my plans for a nap and a quiet morning began to unravel. The dogs started barking and pulling so hard that I needed two people from the village to help me lock them down on the hard-packed snow. We'd just completed an eight-hour run, but the dogs were going ballistic.

Now I was pretty alert, and although I'd had no intention of going further, I started to think about the $3,500 halfway prize at Anvik for the first musher to the Yukon River. It was just another couple of hours on a well-used, hard trail to Anvik, and with the way the team was moving, I thought, "Okay, well, I'll nap later." I had nothing to lose, and the dogs obviously had plenty in reserve.

Our arrival at the checkpoint, signing in, the dogs ramping up, my decision to keep going, and signing out—all of these events happened in a space of eight minutes. My judgment was okay, but I did make a mistake, one that would cost us a couple of hours. The dogs would forgive me, but I'd have to work hard to shake the disappointment in myself.

My only exercise was standing on my drag to slow the team down.

verything was perfect when we left Shageluk and dropped onto the Innoko River. The team and I went by a willow fence frozen into the ice, which directed fish into a trap, and saw the orange-topped surveyor lathe that mark the Iditarod Trail. It was quiet again. The dogs were trotting effortlessly in that steady rhythm, and rocking my sled like a baby cradle.

In my half-sleep state, I thought I was dozing lightly and checking for trail markers. But I wasn't. Forty-five minutes later, I realized we were moving down a slough with just a couple of snowmachine tracks. I had blown it. I'd missed the trail. My heart pounding, I spun the dogs around.

Unbelievable. Agony. Mental torture. I screwed up. As for the dogs, they thought we were going back to the last checkpoint, so they took off like a rocket. I stood on the brake drag, trying to keep the speed down so I wouldn't hurt anybody. We retraced our tracks almost back to Shageluk, the lights of the village visible from the place where I had obviously missed the trail. An **X** of lathe had blocked this side trail, but I hadn't seen it. This time at the fork, I "gee'd" the dogs onto the correct trail to Anvik. In three steps, we went from 15 mph to a very unhappy 5 mph trot.

We were not going to retreat to Shageluk. Even if we had to camp on the trail in complete disgrace, we were going to Anvik. But I'll tell

Finger Lake checkpoint can look like a traffic jam at times. Usually the only winter residents are caretakers at a nearby lodge. JANET TREMER PHOTO

you, I was just sick about two hours turning into four hours. I was in a hopeless, tired state of mind and imagined my young leaders losing all confidence in me: "Lance, it's over. The deal's off." I really thought my race could be over, and watched my team looking back over their shoulders as we went down the trail at half-speed.

Larry still trusted me, but he'd spent his time in front of the team, and at this stage of his life, I could never ask him to lead. I'd done

this once before, so I was really beating myself up. I stopped, snacked the dogs, and apologized a dozen times. "Here, have another slice of lamb. It's my fault."

Eventually we reached the Yukon River, not far from Anvik. It's common to squint your eyes when you're tired, and I've seen things on the ice like a drift log that looks like a boat, light tracers, or ice that looks like an animal. This time, I saw a woman ahead of me. She was sitting beside the trail and not really doing anything except staring at me. The closer I got, the more real she was, and when I passed, she smiled. But when I turned around to wave good-bye, she was gone. I felt I was really awake and had no doubt she was there. It was such a strange experience that it rattled me.

Amazingly the dogs were happy to be in Anvik. They weren't barking, but most of them rolled around on the snow, brushing off the frost, then lapping up their cooked meal. I avoided the dogs and let them rest away from me so they wouldn't feel my disappointment.

After a nap, the world suddenly looked better. Most of the time I'm really happy to be alive, even when I'm screwing up. I figured that the team and I had at least a two- or three-hour time advantage, so we still had some leverage. Of course, time doesn't mean squat if the team loses spirit.

Leaving Anvik, the weather was turning much colder on the Yukon River with a downriver wind in our face. Fortunately, I still had sixteen dogs moving with some raw power, and they had me smiling. They were saying, "Lance, you're forgiven. Just don't do it again."

Bales of straw for bedding are stacked up at the Grayling checkpoint. The Iditarod Trail Committee uses part of our entry fee money to buy and transport straw to the checkpoints. WALT TREMER PHOTO

As the cold started setting in, I was taking precautions for my hands. I just don't have good circulation. Even at 40°F at home, if I don't wear gloves from the time I get out of the truck and walk to the house, they'll be white. With the wind chill on the Yukon, I keep my hands stuffed inside my big mitts, wrapped with three or four activated-carbon hand-warmers.

Usually I can put the pain in the back of my mind. Instead of the dull pain you normally associate with cold hands, I feel sharp pains like a nail's going right through them. I thought amputating my left index finger would resolve the really unbearable pain, but over a couple of years, the same pain has just moved to other fingers. My feet are not so bad.

It took us twelve hours to complete 78 miles of flat trail on the Yukon to the Eagle Island checkpoint. When I finally took my hands out of my mitts, I had to laugh. In the morning light, they were charcoal black from the half-dozen hand warmers I had rolling around in my mitts.

All sixteen dogs were just incredible, but I felt that Chucko, a big two-year-old male, probably had had enough racing. I decided to take him out of the team and let him fly home to Anchorage. "Chucko" was the nickname Conan O'Brien called me when I appeared on his show in New York City. (Incidentally, Conan is just as crazy in person as he is on the show.) Physically, Chucko was perfect, but I expect him to be spectacular as a three-year-old, so I wanted him to remain totally positive.

Meanwhile, Mitch Seavey, the 2004 champ, had made a big move in the pack and arrived next, about three hours after my arrival at Eagle Island. He looked at Chucko barking in the drop-dog area of the Eagle checkpoint and said, "I'll take him in my team." I also got another big surprise from Mitch. I'd sold him a good wheel dog two years earlier, and now Mitch had him in lead. *Wow, that's Molson!* I told Mitch, "Darn it, Mitch, what are you doing with my wheel dog in the lead?"

In Eagle Island, reports from weather-watching pilots predicted that the warm spell was about to end, and a storm was gaining strength. I knew it was going to be tough for my team, but I also knew that the teams behind us might even have it worse. On this section of Yukon River trail, I wasn't giving much of an advantage to other teams, since the wind was just blowing in the trail behind me, covering signs of our progress.

I still had fifteen dogs in harness in the late afternoon of the sixth day of racing. Four front-running teams came into Eagle Island, but I figured they were going to rest and still be four hours behind. I knew that everyone—mushers, officials, and the media—would be looking at my team when we left Eagle Island, looking for evidence that the team might be fading.

For us, it was just a reenactment of a training run on Murphy Dome. The team started out slow, limbering up. That's what they learn to do when you do lots of hook-ups. The first five minutes can be pathetic. I had to look at the far horizon because I didn't want to look at the dogs. I also never looked behind, because I knew Schnuelle, Burmeister, Neff, and Seavey were watching. But I knew in fifteen minutes this team was going to warm up and break some trail like a locomotive, which made me smile. In the checkpoint, the vets gave me a good report and told me the dogs were resting at about 90 beats per minute. By the time we got rolling, their heart rates would be over 300 beats per minute.

In hindsight, I think we were a little ahead of the storm. The wind was strong, especially at a few long river crossings where sandbars were blowing dust, and the trail was filled in with a fine flour snow you always find on the Yukon River. Still, the team was unstoppable, and a little after midnight, we pulled up the slip from the river to the high bank of Kaltag, a village of only about 230 people.

The weather was getting snotty and the visibility was worse. That's why I decided to rest just three hours in Kaltag and get the dogs on the 90-mile portage trail to Unalakleet and the Bering Sea Coast. I was hoping to stay in front of the storm, and I knew the competition behind me was going to get hammered.

My usual routine is to bed the dogs down, check them over with the vets, feed them a hot meal and broth in bowls, and then go into the checkpoint for my own meal. In Kaltag, the eating and sleeping area for the mushers is a log community hall with a big barrel wood stove. After eating, I normally come outside once more to make sure the dogs are lying down and sleeping, then I go back in for my own nap.

But this time, I came out of the community hall to find some of the locals looking at the lead dogs rolling in the snow and barking a little. The rest of the team was sitting up like, "What's up, Lance? Are we leaving? What's the plan?" I haven't figured out a way to tell them to lie down and sleep.

This amazed me, particularly as we got further into the race and the dogs got harder. I was watching this team's power unfold in front of me. Compared to the trouble I had in 2008 with sick dogs not wanting to eat, this team was unbelievable.

I had my plan worked out. The Yukon is a couple of miles wide coming into Kaltag. I knew mushers behind me were going to be right in the middle of a downriver wind. Really there's no protection from the weather when you're on the river ice. It can be demoralizing, so I thought it'd be even better if they came into Kaltag and didn't see or find me. After experiencing the wind of the Yukon, most mushers take a serious look at the weather ahead, especially going into Unalakleet, where a whole new weather system from the Bering Sea can be absolutely deadly vicious.

I was thinking that even if I went 10 miles out of Kaltag on the portage to Unalakleet and camped out for another three hours, that was better than my competition actually seeing me and knowing what I was doing. The dogs were ready and so was I. So we left at about 4:00 A.M. after a three-and-a-half-hour rest.

As it turned out, our little strategy worked. Seavey came into Kaltag an hour and a half later and, of course, didn't see me. He didn't know if I was camped out of the village or trotting straight through to Unalakleet. All he knew was that I wasn't there. I imagined him thinking, "What the heck, Lance left? What are we going to do? The dogs need eight hours' rest, but I guess we'll have to stay six hours and hope he doesn't get away from us. If we don't stay with him, it could be over." To stay with me, they were going to have to rest three and a half hours and follow me, but I figured they wouldn't.

The dogs left really strong out of Kaltag. Other mushers living in Kaltag, like Dean Painter and Richard Burnham, probably gave my competition the full report. I liked that idea. That could be demoralizing along with the weather. So now I was hoping that Seavey, King, Schnuelle, and the others would start thinking about positioning for 2nd place and quit worrying about catching me.

IT SEEMED THE further we got into the race, the stronger the team was getting, picking up little increments of speed, maybe a half-mile an hour faster or even two-tenths of a mile faster than other teams—but it all added up.

As we started to get up in the rolling hills of the coastal range separating Kaltag and Unalakleet, the temperatures began to warm up. It might have been the weather system from the Bering Sea instead of the colder temperatures in the Yukon Basin. I could feel the increase in temperature, so I throttled the dogs back just about a mile an hour. That way they could trot cool and not overexert themselves as we just cruised on in to Unalakleet. It was great, nice and easy, a walk in the park—90 miles at 8.1 mph in about eleven hours.

At Unalakleet, the dogs didn't fool around. They ate, lay down, and went to sleep, something they hadn't done yet on the trail. That told me that they were tired, as they should have been after an eight-hour run into Kaltag and a monster eleven-hour run from Kaltag to Unalakleet. Four hours later, I went out to check on them, and they were sitting up, relaxed, looking things over. That was the same information I was getting all along the trail from people who were keeping an eye on my team as I slept. I knew I was doing something right.

For the first time I was thinking a little bit about Lance, since everything was clicking for the dogs. I was getting a little extra sleep, which was good, because time dedicated to dog maintenance was down. I wasn't worried about wrists and wrapping with neoprene at every checkpoint, dog coats, giving pills to an entire team, or putting ointment on every little rub on the dogs' paws. It was a good run for dog health.

The veterinarians came out and checked the dogs. The splits on two dogs were just about healed. I was on top of that. Nobody was sick, no antibiotics, and no medications. I still had fifteen dogs and felt like team health was remarkable—even if they were mine.

As required gear for vet checks, mushers carry waterproof field notebooks for the veterinarians to record their observations at the checkpoints. They're similar to the yellow notebooks you see surveyors or engineers use on the job. The pages list the dogs and provide space for the veterinarians to write details. In the space marked for overall condition of the team at Unalakleet, my vet book said "Perfect."

It's hard to imagine that resting in an arctic wind on the ice of the Unalakleet River for seven hours and seven minutes would be sufficient to crank up a team that had just traveled 862 miles in the last eight days. But that rest in the village ignited my team like a stick of dynamite. The dogs worked together up the Blueberry Hills to Shaktoolik and gave me a beautiful night ride. My only exercise was standing on my drag to slow the team down

But on this leg of the race, I got cold, really cold. I haven't been that miserable for a long time—or ever. The temperature had dropped to -30°F and that constant Bering Sea wind just took it out of me. The wind was right in my face. I couldn't turn well enough to block it with my parka ruff and still keep running and working to keep ahead of the cold. No matter how much I moved, I just couldn't get warm. I had to think about keeping my water bottle thawed out, eating enough snacks, and ensuring I had circulation in my hands. Still I felt frozen by the time we dropped out of the hills. We traveled the last 12 miles on freshwater sloughs and a trail following the beach dune line into Shaktoolik.

I never intended to stay in Shaktoolik. Strategywise it did not make sense, even with a five- or six-hour lead. I did not want those guys behind me to even know we existed. My main thought was just

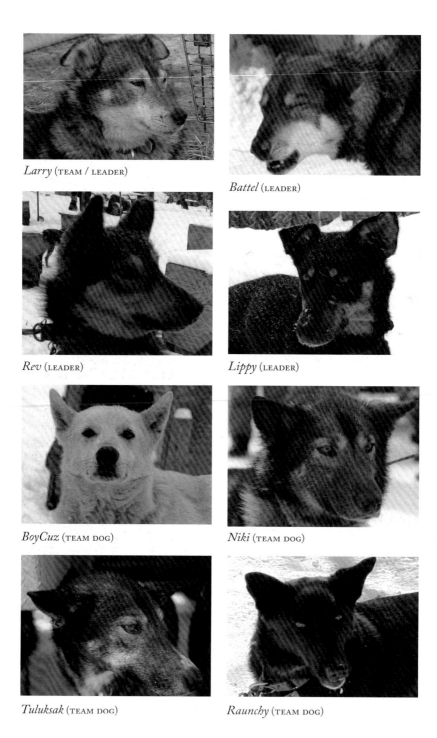

Larry (TEAM / LEADER)

Battel (LEADER)

Rev (LEADER)

Lippy (LEADER)

BoyCuz (TEAM DOG)

Niki (TEAM DOG)

Tuluksak (TEAM DOG)

Raunchy (TEAM DOG)

Visit us at www.mackeyscomebackkennel.com
to see who's on tap for this year's team.

Maple (LEADER)

Zena (LEADER)

Dred (LEADER)

Rapper (WHEEL DOG)

Chucko (TEAM DOG)

Shasta (TEAM DOG)

Pimp (WHEEL DOG)

Pauly (WHEEL / TEAM)

to get out of Shaktoolik—and out of the minds of Seavey, Neff, Burmeister, Baker, Schnuelle, and King.

But more importantly, I had to pay attention to this little problem of staying alive. I had not dressed for the wind and this level of cold. I tucked the dogs out of the howling wind beside the steel National Guard building that was the checkpoint. I didn't take off their booties while I went inside to reorganize for the 58-mile trip to Koyuk.

I was all alone and going into a storm that was getting worse by the minute. If I got stuck out there, the Eskimo guys in Shaktoolik were not going to start looking for me until the storm settled down. Besides, if it's a whiteout, you can't see anyway. I had to be self-contained. We were leading, which was good, but we were all alone, and it wouldn't be wise to start out already cold. Nobody's died on the Iditarod, but some have come close to it.

Inside the checkpoint, I stripped down to my underwear. My boots were frosted up and frozen. I took the liners out of my overshoes, and put them on a big oil heater to dry along with my pants and parka—about everything I was wearing was damp. I brought out some of my cold-weather gear, including some caribou socks and windbreakers to put over my pants and parka. I was looking at gear closely because I was thinking we may not make it through this storm today. My water bottles were frozen. I refilled them so I'd have plenty of water in case we had to sit on the ice in a storm. My thermos was topped off with hot water.

Finally, I was starting to feel better—a lot better. I ate a hot meal and put on my dry clothes, plus my pullover parka, and windbreakers. Inside my boots were my caribou slippers for extra protection. My feet were really hurting in a sharp way.

The checkpoint volunteers and local people were great and totally supportive. They were true Eskimos, who lived understanding the wind. It took me thirty-seven minutes to check in and out of Shaktoolik, and every minute getting warm was worth it.

The trail out of Shaktoolik crosses frozen sloughs and tundra to the ice of Norton Sound. It is featureless and absolutely flat except for drifts and upended ice. In a whiteout, it's hard to tell if you are on freshwater ice, tundra, or sea ice, except for an occasional dry blade of grass or brush coming up through the hard pack. After about 12 miles, the trail passes a shelter cabin near a big rock bluff called Island Point. Once you go by the shelter cabin, you're on the sea ice of Norton Sound for real, and there's no place to hide until you get to Koyuk 40 miles later.

If the storm was too much to battle, or if the wind blew out the Iditarod Trail markers (definitely a possibility), I could always stay at the shelter cabin. The locals told me it had been rebuilt recently and had a good wood stove. I have been through this drill before and was a little skeptical. Just to get a confirmation, I'd asked several people if there was any wood at the shelter cabin. I started joking around, "Who cares about the stove? There isn't a stick of wood around for miles, so somebody had to haul wood to the cabin." Yes, the locals told me, firewood was there at the shelter. Just to double check, I asked another villager, "You know anything about any wood out there at the shelter cabin?" and finally I was convinced that I could count on it for warmth and shelter from the wind. I've heard some mushers call the place Lonely Rock, because it's the only feature for miles.

WHEN I PULLED the team out from behind the checkpoint building, the wind and drift hit us head-on. Literally, it was breathtaking. Nothing in my young leaders' experience could prepare them for this moment. They just stood there in disbelief. That's when I knew it was Larry time. I took the old dog from his protected spot and put him in the lead for the first time. Without hesitation, Larry leaned into the wind and led us onto the ice. I was flushed with pride.

The dogs were unbelievable. From time to time, one of the superstars would wind up and hammer the harness at a run, trying to get the team to go faster. Regardless of the powerful gusting winds, we made good time. As we traveled, I thought about how Joe Garnie once told me the wind is not always constant—sometimes you can wait and it will lay down. Then you move, and if it pins you down

Larry got us through the toughest stretches of trail, and they were fifteen strong as we approached Nome—I couldn't ask for more. AL GRILLO PHOTO

again, just wait and do it over again. Sometimes you can work yourself out of a blowhole, those areas where the wind blows so hard you can't even stand up.

I could see the bright orange shelter cabin for quite a ways through the blowing snow. I started thinking, "Ah, we made it, we made it, we made it." The dogs were knifing through the wind, and it seemed visibility was better than I thought. As we got closer to the little cabin, I debated with myself about stopping, "Should I? Should I? Should I?" Then we were passing it, and I was saying, "Screw it, we're going to Koyuk!"

To the east, a wall of weather was forming almost before my eyes. It was tough going for us in the wind, basically just working our way from trail marker to marker for 40 miles. The ground storm created a whiteout and plastered a rim of snow around the dogs' eyes. I stopped often to rub their muzzles and eyes with my mitts, while looking ahead for another trail marker reflector to flash in my headlight. As hard as it was, I think we were lucky, staying on the edge of the storm while mushers behind us had an even tougher time.

As we approached Koyuk, 171 miles from the finish, the wind finally laid down a little. It was still a consideration, but it wasn't anything like the storm we faced leaving the shelter cabin. At the checkpoint, I noted our run time on the checker's sheet—7 hours and 2 minutes— and told the official, "Those guys are going to have a tough time getting through that storm. I don't think anybody is going to beat that time." We may have been going only 8 mph, but it was under extraordinary conditions, and every dog in my fifteen was pulling.

The dog team was a dream. Even after that gnarly, windblown, miserable ride of 98 miles from Unalakleet to Shaktoolik and then over the ice to Koyuk, most of the dogs were still banging their harness and barking to go. The fans, the officials, and the baffled veterinarians were all talking about the durability and health of the team.

At Koyuk, race sponsor Anchorage Chrysler Dodge had set up a shelter tent as a checkpoint work area for the veterinarians. I parked the dogs as close to the tent as possible. My biggest problem was kids throwing snowballs, yelling, screaming, sledding, and running around the dogs. That eventually settled down, but I can also say my dogs were relaxed enough to handle it.

By habit I came out of the checkpoint building every couple of hours to check on the dogs or bring them another hot meal. Each time, I looked back on the sea ice for a musher. Nothing. Meanwhile nearly five hours had passed, and everybody was getting conflicting reports about what was happening behind me—the radio operator, the officials, locals who had relatives and friends in Shaktoolik. Apparently, there was chaos on the trail. Some reports said that teams were out, but were stuck in the wind at the shelter cabin, and other teams were turning back to Shaktoolik. I heard that Dallas Seavey, the nationally ranked wrestler and twenty-one-year-old son of Iditarod champ Mitch Seavey, was now suddenly in the Top 5. I kept wondering, "What the hell is going on back there?"

My dogs were getting lots of rest and eating—inhaling—snacks and meals. We had arrived at noon, which is perfect timing, because they can rest in the afternoon sun. With only 171 miles to go, people started acting like it was a foregone conclusion that the race was in the bag. A couple of them started asking me what color truck I was going to order this year from Anchorage Chrysler Dodge. "Whoa, whoa, hold on there!" was my answer. I was still nervous about the weather, and I wasn't traveling in a buddy system with another team who'd help find the trail. All alone at the front makes you extra-cautious.

Finally, by evening, Sebastian Schnuelle arrived in Koyuk after a long, tough run from Unalakleet. Schnuelle's arrival was my alarm clock. By the time I got the dogs bootied and the sled loaded with lots of extra food, it was almost 9:00 P.M. The dogs had rested for almost nine hours!

To my surprise, the team was sluggish leaving Koyuk. Then Maple, my young female leader, veered off the trail on a wild snowmachine track. She wasn't an experienced command leader, and this wasn't the time for a big discussion with Maple on which trail we were taking. Again I brought good old trusty Larry out of the team for some select duty. Of course, he follows voice commands cross-country, and he took control until we intercepted the trail again. All it took was a couple of "haw" commands, busting through some drifts and brush, and Larry had us pointed in the right direction.

For the first time in the race, I saw some emotion from Larry. He was happy now in the lead. I'd noticed that he'd been kind of "doing his job" above the wheel—not pouting—but just putting his time in. He was such a good leader and a proud animal that I could understand how he felt back in front of the team.

When we left Koyuk, reports had indicated -20°F ambient temperatures and a -50°F wind chill. It was tough. Schnuelle said he probably would never have gone on the ice at Shaktoolik if he'd have known the winds were so fierce. Following Schnuelle was John Baker, an Iñpuiaq from Kotzebue, who trains in bad weather all the time. He was next in line, in large part, because his dogs knew how to go through the wind. Baker was also a pilot, so I believed it when he later said winds were 50-plus mph in some spots on Norton Sound.

The weather that Joe Garnie had predicted was real. And yet as hard as I'd prepared, there's nothing like the actual encounter with weather. Even so, when my vision was completely wiped out by a white sheet of blowing snow, even the young leaders had an instinct for following the established trail. I believe they not only see better than we do, especially at night, but they combine that sense with smell and the feel of the trail under their feet.

I was extremely careful to move from trail marker to marker on the 48-mile night run to Elim, always keeping an Iditarod reflector in sight. I can honestly say that run was tougher than the ice on Norton Sound. On one occasion, we were bouncing over hard-packed waves of snow when the wind hit us from the side and drove the team, sled, and me off the hill into a thicket of willows. We got out and back on the trail, but not without effort.

THROUGHOUT THE RACE, but especially during these side adventures, I was keenly aware of working around my physical limitations. For one, I just could not let my hands get cold. It would take me hours to warm up again, and I wouldn't be doing anybody any good if I couldn't even help myself. Most mushers can fool with booties with their bare hands or a thin pair of gloves. I have my booties designed extra large, so I can put them on with heavy gloves. Velcro fastens the booties around the dog's "wrist," so I have them made extra long so I can grab them with my mitts in a storm. It probably slows my dogs a little, but I have to do it.

I also breed and train exceptional, athletic dogs. But if they're not able to relax and let me handle them with my limitations, I have to sell them to other mushers. All my dogs have to "melt" to me and trust me, even in a blowing storm. In the end, thinking so much about overcoming my limitations probably makes me a better musher.

Despite getting blown off the trail, we were still in the lead, but I wasn't ready to celebrate just yet. Not when I was followed by a pack of mushers who each understood the law of this trail: all it takes is one mistake, one missed turn, to give away a race. With a cushion of over six hours, I was really focusing on not screwing up on the final leg to White Mountain.

At the little village of Golovin, a crowd had gathered to congratulate the team and even to collect autographs. My dad had summer work here years ago, managing a fish-processing operation, so a number of the older Native people approached me with a warm, "Welcome home, Lance." It felt good.

Eighteen miles later, I heard a church bell ringing in the cold air as the dogs trotted like rockets into White Mountain, a beautiful village set on a hillside overlooking the Fish River. We were met by a crowd of fans, locals, and media. I chatted a little as I got to work bedding down the dogs and firing up my cooker to make them a big, hot meal. But I wasn't too busy to notice a familiar face in the crowd, someone who was hanging back. And what a surprise it was—my mother, who'd flown out from Nome!

"What are you doing here, Mom?" I gave her a big hug. Here she was, the woman who'd never asked for any credit in my mushing career, going the extra mile again. I, for one, would never forget her part in making sure we had sled dogs when I was a kid. And both of us had tackled and beat cancer, too. We never talked about it really, but I think we both understood how that battle seems to sharpen your focus and make all life events more important.

Fans and reporters were talking to me like the race was in the bag. I had fifteen dogs, which to my knowledge was the biggest string of any front-runner in Iditarod history. And I had a seven-hour advantage over Schnuelle. But all I had to do was perform a history-making screw-up, and he could steal the race.

I left White Mountain with both good and bad thoughts. This was the final run of a race hammered by brutal weather—the worst I had seen in my career. The 77 miles into Nome are legendary for blowholes. And then there's the climb up the notorious Topkok Hill, a mountain that has disoriented even local mushers for more than a century.

Once we summited and then dropped off Topkok to a shelter cabin at the base of the mountain, I still had watch to watch for blowholes on the trail to Nome, especially a famous one that whistles off the mountains at Solomon. You can hit 80-mph wind anywhere,

It's so heart-warming to see my great fans. Janet Tremer photo

but that place is famous for it. I felt lucky to have dog power, probably more than any front-running musher.

One other bad thought was nagging me, though. This was the same section of trail where that drunken snowmachiner had mowed down my team and damn near killed Zorro and me. Some of the dogs in the team remembered it, too, as we neared Nome. They started reacting to the whine of snowmachines. Rather than working straight ahead, they were nervously shifting gait, thinking about an exit strategy in case a snowmachine came closer. I started to consider what I would do if they decided to lay down. Fortunately, none of the machines came close, possibly as a result of a safety campaign in Nome.

And then it was over—the planning and strategizing, the balancing act of warmth and calories, the gambling over weather conditions, the anticipation born of a series of good decisions—it ended the moment I stepped off the runners. We arrived under the Burled Arch after a long, very physical race at 11:38 A.M., March 18, to win the 2009 race, my third consecutive Iditarod championship. Our trail time was 9 days, 21 hours, 38 minutes, and 46 seconds.

Sebastian Schnuelle, who'd just won the 2009 Yukon Quest a few weeks earlier, finished in second place, seven and a half hours later after running a good race of his own. John Baker, the Kotzebue man, worked his magic and drove his dogs through the Bering Sea storm to finish in 3rd.

As for the good thoughts, they were really good. My wife, Tonya, family, and friends were set to have fun celebrating this win. Finishing with fifteen healthy dogs on an unusually tough trail was so satisfying. No denying it, I also felt some enjoyment knowing the detractors—those who'd said I was a fluke and would never win a third straight Iditarod—ate a little crow.

Just as I crossed the finish line, somebody handed me a telephone. No, it wasn't the governor on the line. It was Dad calling from Arizona. Long trips are getting a little tougher for him, but he was still there with me. It was almost comical—there I was, surrounded by a crowd and television cameras at the finish, and Dad was saying, "Good job, Lance!" and wanting to know every detail of the race. I had to tell him, "Dad, I'll call back in a few minutes."

On the platform under the arch, I sat with the dogs while multiple camera floodlights and flashes lit up the night, so bright it seemed like midday. I hugged my leaders and spoke from the heart when I said, "If you're gonna dream, dream big, right?"

One of my goals it to prove to the world that the job of a sled dog gives them self-worth. That's why I don't take any of that away from the dogs, even in the yard. One of my most exciting moments in the sport was receiving the 2009 Alaska Airlines Leonhard Seppala Humanitarian Award, given to a Top 20 team that satisfies health and condition criteria established by the Iditarod veterinarians. It's a big deal to receive this honor because there isn't anything political about it—it all comes from the history written in those notebooks we carry as a mandatory piece of gear throughout the race. If you have the most well-cared-for team in the race, you get the lead crystal cup mounted on a wood base, plus a couple of round-trip tickets from Alaska Airlines.

The team was still in race mode when we charged down Front Street to the Burled Arch for a third consecutive victory. AL GRILLO PHOTO

Maple and Larry were oblivious to the crowds. To them, stopping in a checkpoint means time for a nap. JANET TREMER PHOTO

The three-peat was sweet. To win under such extreme conditions with a wide margin and the largest team ever to cross the finish line—I was so proud of the team. The icing on the cake was the incredible honor of winning the Humanitarian Award.

My thoughts flew back to last spring, when I was sitting out in the dog yard in the sun, staring at the dogs as I pondered this very race. It seemed yet another dream had come true.

We have decided to set the goal fairly high.

npredictability and uncertainty always figures in my race strategy, so I admit it's probably part of my outlook in life. Of course, I don't know what the future's going to bring, but I do have this ongoing anxiety about using time and not wasting an opportunity to accomplish my goals. Thankfully, my family and friends tolerate behavior that sometimes seems fixated on a narrow view of life.

My son, Cain, usually monitors my cell phone at the house when I'm training the dogs. I get reports all the time, some of them pretty humorous, from friends who try to call me and get Cain's "Hello?"

"Is that you, Cain?" they'll ask.

"Yeah, I'm answering Lance's phone," explains my volunteer call-screener.

"Can I talk to Lance?" That's logical. Somebody wants to talk to me.

Cain starts chuckling, "Are you kidding me? Lance is out training dogs. You might catch him tomorrow night for a couple of hours, but that's not for sure."

I'm not intentionally avoiding anyone, but my focus is training the team, and if I paused for every call, I'd never get anywhere. During training season, I'm hard to contact at home and pretty much impossible to catch on the trail. But most of my family and other people who help me already understand that my job starts for real on September 1, seven days a week, all day, until the snow is gone in early April. During those months I rarely watch television, don't catch the news, and outside of my interest in the dogs and my family, I don't see what's going on in the rest of the world. Fortunately, I have group of loyal friends, from my fans to my accountant to my doctors to my lawyer, who filter the outside world for me. Ninety percent of the messages to me go through Tonya or our good friend and my agent, Theresa Daily. They keep my Web page current, handle orders for sweatshirts and Larry and Zorro patches, answer questions from fans, or find somebody who can speak for me. I may not answer every letter, but I know that every fan is going to get some attention from my camp.

When I get off a training run, I can expect to look through a pile of information, bills, or important messages. I'll find a week's worth to review in a couple of hours, because I'll be leaving again for my little world with the team.

How's my passion for the sport? It's as strong as ever, and you can't say something like that without really meaning it. Somebody will know you're faking. I am so in love with what I do, yet I also realize my focus probably borders on the obsessive. I pawn off so many responsibilities to my many great friends—I know I miss a lot of a normal person's reality. I've learned to pay the winter's bills in advance, now that we can manage it, so I don't have to think about them. And Cain is nearly out of high school, but I'm unaware of many events in his life. So I understand that my fixation on mushing and commitment takes a price, and just have to hope that he understands I'm thinking of him.

For the immediate future, I'm really interested in what's going to happen in 2010 in the world of long-distance sled-dog racing. Some of my competitors in the Yukon Quest, including names like Sebastian Schnuelle, Hans Gatt, and my neighbor Ken Anderson, have adopted the idea of long runs as central to their race strategies. They've already tried what I've done by running two 1,000-mile races in a month, and they've learned how that develops incredible endurance animals. Other mushers like Martin Buser or Mitch Seavey, who have well-

Getting busy on the Gin Gin 200. I was fortunate to win 1st place again in 2009.
THERESA DAILY PHOTO

established kennels, are also considering putting teams in both the Yukon Quest and the Iditarod for 2010 races.

What they have to learn is where the red line is on their team's performance. The dogs are quite willing to travel way above that line, so it's the musher's job to slow them down and keep the team's physical strength in reserve. Just as bicycle riders and marathon runners have learned to pace themselves over weeks of racing, we're all learning to sustain that speed day after day. Of course, you now know that for me, planning and practicing for every contingency wraps around this primary strategy.

In 2010, the race calendar is on my side for running both the Yukon Quest and the Iditarod in the same year. The Yukon Quest starts February 6, 2010. Though that early February start in Whitehorse, Canada, almost guarantees some brutally cold weather, when you figure a ten-day race, we'll be resting on February 16. The Iditarod always starts on the first Saturday of March, which falls on March 6. That means I'll have almost three weeks to recuperate and organize between the finish of the Quest and the start of the Iditarod. So, you bet, I plan on racing both of Alaska's long-distance races.

I spent a lot of time standing on the hill overlooking the dog yard during the summer of 2009, gazing at the endless Alaskan wilderness to the horizon, thinking about my new team for the next year. I finished with fifteen dogs in the 2009 Iditarod, but one of them is probably retired from my team. My great leader Larry, now nine years old, would likely have a tough time keeping up with my new lineup of fast travelers. Larry is still a key player at the kennel, however, and he can lead and train a second team of young prospects through storms and over rough country, but at a slower pace. The next time, the young leaders will do it on their own.

Two dogs from the winning 2009 team belonged to Joe Garnie, and they'll be back with him in the village of Teller. That leaves me a core of twelve proven, veteran dogs from that team that are ready to race in 2010. And in reserve are twenty-two dogs just two years old

that raced with Braxton, Cain, and Harry Alexie in the preseason races. Now they're experienced and physically mature. Harry has also raced the Iditarod and finished with ten dogs, so I count those dogs in the group of veterans, too.

We started in the fall of 2009 with sixty dogs that I thought could race at a championship level. By New Year's, we had narrowed the field to forty-seven dogs. Out of that group, fourteen dogs will go into my Yukon Quest team and leave a reserve group in training to fill out my Iditarod team of sixteen.

Three generations of winners at Iditarod Headquarters: Cain Carter, Lance Mackey and Dick Mackey. THERESA DAILY PHOTO

A second team of dogs will then be available for Newton Marshall, a friend of mine with an incredible story in the world of sled-dog mushing. Newton was all over the news in Alaska when it was announced that he would be running a team of Iditarod dogs from Mackey's Comeback Kennel, plus training and living with me on Murphy Dome Road. Newton is from Jamaica and a member of the Jamaican Dogsled Team, which races on dry land. The unusual team was founded by Danny Melville, an adventure tour operator in the Caribbean, and sponsored by entertainer Jimmy Buffett. Of course, Jimmy loves the Caribbean and Jamaica and just got an immense kick out of the idea of a Jamaican running competitively in the Iditarod. That's where I come in.

Newton Marshall has already proven that he's the real deal as a musher. In 2009 he trained with Quest champion Hans Gatt in Canada, then finished with a solid 13th place in the 2009 Yukon Quest. That totally qualifies him to enter the 2010 as a rookie. Newton is a great guy, totally Jamaican, loves reggae music, athletic, and is going with me on every training and camping expedition. He may take Larry as leader—we'll have to wait and see what Larry decides.

Coming off the 2009 season with some success, plus having that pool of veterans and some good young dogs, my confidence level has come up a bit. I think I have the knowledge and ability to put together a good team. If I just hold them together, I think it will be okay.

I like to visualize that I could have two teams in place, one for each of the two big races. But for the last four years I've said that, and it's never worked out. I have enough dogs for two separate teams, but it sure would be hard to leave behind some of what I think are my best dogs. So I'm planning on just taking my most exceptional fourteen dogs on the Yukon Quest, especially since the competition is going to be stiff. Hopefully, I'll have fourteen that are fired up for the Iditarod three weeks later, but realistically, I'll probably have ten or twelve from the Yukon Quest team. That means we'll fill out the team with four to six more from the reserves that Braxton is training.

Of course, some of my Quest dogs could very easily go with Newton on his Iditarod team instead.

One of the most exciting considerations for the future is how to handle the really exceptional, unbelievable hard drivers that are coming out of the newest groups of pups. Genetically, some of them are physically incredible. Naturally I'm hoping that my methods of encouraging them as pups will help them develop their full abilities. Two are absolute rockets. They're brothers named Amp and Von, out of my young leader Rev, who is out of Zorro. They have no thousand-mile experience, but they've run in 200- and 300-mile races, so I'm keeping my fingers crossed. I love the anticipation of watching young dogs mature, but I let their performance do the bragging. We'll see how they do.

As for leaders, I have to admit that the kennel is transforming, and I haven't found another leader like Larry. Maple could be that exceptional leader, but none of them has emerged in a dramatic way to take over Larry's position. In 2010, we may face another storm, and Larry won't be there to lead us out of Shaktoolik in a headwind. I don't know which leader will take that job, but I know it will happen.

In truth, my team has really changed personality, and I have the challenge of managing some real drivers that just lean into the harness as hard as they can. A big decision for me for the 2010 season is who to key off for my team governor. Every musher's dream is to think all night about a team of hard-driving, out-of-their-minds dogs, barking and banging their harness all the way to Nome. But here I am thinking about slowing them down!

Larry told me to peg the team to his speed in 2009. For most of the race, he never led in front of the team, but he was the "leader." In a couple of emergencies, I pulled him out of the line-up and put him to the front and he put the team back on the trail. Having established that Larry is retired, I looked over the yard all summer, looking for another dog to help me—to be the one that I key off for the overall good of the team.

That's going to require a lot thinking to get it right. This year the team is going to have lots of speed, and I really have to be careful about letting them scorch the trail. I'm seriously considering Rapper to set the team speed. He's a solid male out of Zorro, and though he's not the fastest dog, I think his common sense makes him a good pacesetter. The problem with him is his preference to run in the back of the team closer to the sled, even in the wheel. But it doesn't really matter, because I can watch him anywhere and let him set the point for his comfort level.

One spring day after the 2009 Iditarod, I got a visit from George Attla, the legendary musher who once dominated the world of sled-dog sprint racing. When he was Alaska's most famous musher, winning the biggest sprint races in 1970, I was riding the runners as an unborn baby with my mother. He was born in 1933, so our careers are a little out of sync. George is an Athabascan Indian from the Koyukuk River, a tributary of the Yukon. He was also made famous by a great movie about his life titled *Spirit of the Wind*. I just think George Attla is awesome, and I love talking to him. It was an unusual honor when he and his son came to buy a dog. Right away, I said, "George, why'd you come to my house? These dogs don't move that fast!" Well, he wanted a dog. He came and visited several times, and even though the dog yard was rearranged on his return visits, with dogs in different spots, he kept going back to the same dogs—my hard chargers. I don't know if he'd just memorized the dogs, or he looked at the way they were built and the way they moved. He told me, "Lance, you could win the Fur Rendezvous with these dogs." We both knew he was talking about the highlight of Anchorage's winter carnival, the fast and furious sprint run known as Fur Rendezvous World Championship Sled Dog Race.

On another trip out, I told him, "George, go ahead and pick out a dog, and see if you like the genetics." He chose a little female for his son's kennel. It was a great honor. Truthfully, if it wasn't for me clamping down on the team's speed, I believe George was right. Those hard drivers in my team would be all-purpose and fast enough to race the Fur Rendezvous for 30 miles of all-out speed.

So I have a good group. But I am realistic and know the problems will be there to overcome.

As for my personal health issues, I like to see everything as a natural process of aging for a normal forty-year-old male. That puts it into perspective for me. This is how my aging process is going: during the last forty years of life, banging my right arm on car doors and flipping with sleds, I developed two bone chips at my elbow. The chips could have originated in my elbow or actually migrated from somewhere else on my arm. One chip was lodged at the elbow, while the other was fused to bone on my forearm. The bone on my forearm was fairly painful, like a rock in your shoe that never goes away, especially when I bent my arm to put on my coat or lift up a bag of dog food. It felt like I could just make an incision and simply remove the bone fragments.

When I finally saw a doctor in the fall of 2009, he agreed and said, "Yes, that's exactly what we'll do, but it's more of a hospital procedure." The plan was to knock me out in a hospital setting and treat it like a normal surgery.

"Well, I'm not going to do that," I said. "I've been put under too many times. This is just too minor. Let's do it in the clinic." Well, I think that surprised the doctor, but he said okay, we'll do it your way. So I jumped on the table, and we did it with local anesthesia in the clinic. Since it was kind of unusual, he brought in another physician and staff person. They put a tourniquet above and below my elbow and did just what I envisioned by plucking out the chips. No fuss, no muss, no big deal.

Two days later, I flew to Toronto, Canada, for a fund-raiser benefitting the Jamaican Dogsled Team. It included a big Jimmy Buffett concert and a showing of *Underdog*, a documentary about Newton Marshall's 2009 Yukon Quest. I was going to meet everybody, including the team founder Danny Melville, Jimmy Buffett, and Newton Marshall. And I was supposed to speak at the premiere festivities.

I thought I was recovering well, and pain is something I can always put in the background. However, air pressure changes during the flight had caused my arm to swell—and I mean from the tips of my fingers to my armpit—to the size of a tree trunk. My doctor warned me it could happen, but I thought it was a little dark humor and didn't take him seriously. Three days later I saw the doctor back in Fairbanks, and he worked to get the swelling down. It turned out that a fluid pocket about the size of a baseball remained in my elbow.

I had seen it done on dogs, so I decided to save on medical expenses—which are trying to wipe me out—and remove the fluid myself at home with a syringe, then take antibiotics, all of which I have right in the kitchen. Apparently, I infected the elbow in the process of doctoring myself. Two days later it looked pretty serious. I'd developed a massive staph infection, and for a while it looked like I might lose my right arm. Fortunately, the doctor saved me by cleaning out the elbow, more extensive than the original procedure, and installing a drip antibiotic pump. I had to make daily visits to the clinic.

In the end, I lost all of November training time, which was tough. Instead, I spent it on the couch staring out the window, not even able to tie my shoelaces. Once again I was depending on others to do my work. This time it wasn't my daughters, but rather Cain and Braxton out there. Ultimately, I didn't save on a medical bill, but I think the arm is loosening up and I'll be all right.

Until then, my knee had been a bigger priority than my arm. Now it's reminding me that it's the number-one issue again. As I prepare for the 2010 season, I'm wearing a brace and getting some kind of liquid cartilage injections to keep me going through the season. I should have it replaced immediately, but I'm putting it off for just a few more months. I've had lengthy discussions with my doctor about available procedures, and we're planning on a total knee replacement in the summer.

In summary, I am a physical train wreck, even aside from the effects of my radiation treatment for cancer, the elbow, the knee, my deteriorating teeth—or lack of them—my jaw and the sensitive tissue on the right side of my neck, my right arm, the missing finger, poor circulation in my feet and hands, and the chronic pain, which I just ignore. From the long view, it's kind of comical. I just have to laugh.